Kenneth W. Ford
UNIVERSITY OF MASSACHUSETTS AT BOSTON

Answer Manual to Accompany

Volume 1

Classical and Modern Physics

A TEXTBOOK FOR STUDENTS OF SCIENCE AND ENGINEERING

This manual was prepared with the assistance of

Eric Dietz
Costas Papanicolas
and
Peter Rapidis

XEROX COLLEGE PUBLISHING *Lexington, Massachusetts | Toronto*

ISB Number: 0-536-00867-1

Printed in the United States of America.

FORWARD

This manual contains answers to exercises, problems, and selected questions. In some instances, supplementary information related to an answer or to a method of solution is also provided; such information appears in parentheses. Additional remarks of amplification or clarification appear occasionally and are enclosed in brackets. Vectors are indicated by wavy underlining corresponding to boldface in the text.

Numerical answers are given most often to three significant figures, sometimes to two or four figures. Usually the accuracy expected in students' answers will be somewhat less than the accuracy appearing in the manual. Numerical values in the exercises and problems are always chosen to be realistic but only rarely are chosen to simplify arithmetic. Every student should be encouraged to become adept with a slide rule--unless he or she is fortunate enough to have ready access to a desk calculator.

Despite the best efforts of those of us working on this manual, some errors have undoubtedly crept into it. I will be most grateful to instructors who call my attention to any wrong answers or ambiguous questions.

In addition to the collaborators (Eric Dietz, Costas Papanicolas, and Peter Rapidis), I have had considerable help from Dale Tong, who provided answers to many of the exercises and problems. Elizabeth Higgins typed the manual--conscientiously and expertly.

Kenneth W. Ford

CHAPTER 1

Q1.3 Man's complexity is the key. Thousands of atoms may be needed to construct a single molecule of living matter, a vast number of molecules is needed to make a single cell, innumerable cells to make a single organ.

Q1.4 Mechanics, thermodynamics, electromagnetism.

Q1.7 Statement (1) is typical scientific explanation; it specifies the microscopic basis of a macroscopic fact. Statement (3) is either explanation (of the process of burning) or definition (of the word "burning").

Q1.13 Space flight itself is primarily a technological achievement; it becomes a tool of scientific research.

Q1.18 Most physicists would probably answer in the negative, but some (such as Eugene Wigner) have argued for the affirmative.*

. . . .

E1.1 (a) 10. (b) 5×10^{15}. (c) 6.3×10^{7}. (d) 3.3×10^{-7}.

E1.2 (a) 10^4 years. (b) 10^7 years. (c) 10^{10} years.

E1.3 (a) 10^{-22} sec. (b) 10^{-18} sec. (c) 10^{-15} sec.

E1.4 (a) 10^{14} sec, or 3.2×10^6 years. (b) 10^{12} nuclei. (c) 10^5.

E1.5 Nuclear diameter would be about 10^{-4} m, or 0.1 mm (0.2 mm is acceptable, since student might take the numbers in Table 1.1 to be radii). Yes, he would fit between earth and sun (180 cm would stretch to 0.12 A.U.).

E1.7 (1) About 10^{82} particles. (2) About 10^{12} m, comparable to the dimension of a large star.

. . . .

P1.1 Height $h = \alpha t^2$.

Rocket	α	Height h at t = 25 sec
A	5 ft/sec^2	3,125 ft
B	4×10^{-3} mile/sec^2	2.5 miles
C	3.64 (±0.01) m/sec^2	2,275 (±6) m

*See E. P. Wigner, Symmetries and Reflections (Indiana University Press, 1967), pp. 211-221.

CHAPTER 2

Q2.2 (a), (c), (g). Only the very unusual student will know that disorder (g) can be a quantitative concept. It is inserted here to stimulate discussion and learning, not to test knowledge. Note that galaxy (e) might be a unit of measurement but is not a quantitative concept as defined in the chapter. Atomic energy (f) as it is usually used is not a quantitative concept, but it could be. The same applies to progress (d).

Q2.3 (1), (3), (4).

Q2.6 No. Distinct concepts (such as energy and torque) may have the same dimension.

Q2.7 (1) No. (2) Yes.

Q2.13 (1) Triangulation from different points on Earth. (2) Radar or laser reflection. For the latter method, the speed of light must be known.

Q2.14 Not operational and not satisfactory.

Q2.15 Mass is proportional to volume, which scales as the cube of the linear dimension.

Q2.19 Both particles gain speed in the collision.

Q2.23 (1) Greater with respect to the sun. (2) More nearly constant with respect to the earth.

Q2.24 Length (space) and time; force; speed, momentum, and energy of a free particle.

. . . .

E2.1 (1) 3.3×10^{-19} sec. (2) (a) 1.80×10^{11} m. (b) 1.12×10^{8} miles. (3) $c = 9.84\times10^{8}$ ft/sec = 1.86×10^{5} mile/sec = 6.71×10^{8} mile/hr = 300 m/μsec.

E2.2 (a) 62.14 mile/hr. (b) 109.36 yards. (c) 804.67 m. (d) 0.1 J.

E2.3 (a) 2.99×10^{8} m/sec. (b) 0.9144 m. (c) 9.75 m/sec^2.

E2.4 (1) 10^3 kg/m^3. (2) 3.79×10^{-3} m^3/gallon, or 264 gallon/m^3. [<u>Note</u>: Early printings of the book give the crude approximation 8 lb/gallon for the density of water. This leads to 3.63×10^{-3} m^3/gallon, or 276 gallon/m^3.]

E2.6 ML^2T^{-3}. kg m^2/sec^3, or J/sec, or W.

E2.7 Let V represent speed. (a) LV^{-1}. (b) $L^{-1}V^2$.

E2.8 Let A represent acceleration. (a) AT^2. (b) AT.

E2.9 $FM^{-1}T^2$ (F represents force).

E2.10 N m^2/kg^2, or m^3/kg sec^2.

E2.11 $ML^{-1}T^{-1}$. kg/m sec (or N sec/m^2).

E2.12 (a) 6.324×10^4 A.U./light-year.
(b) 1.467 (ft/sec)/(mile/hr).

E2.15 (1) P = 4M (P = price in dollars, M = mass in kg).
(2) P = CM (C expressed in price/mass).

E2.16 (a), (e), (f), (h).

E2.17 (b), (c), (e).

E2.18 Less than 1 mile (0.932 mile). 3.73 min, or 3 min, 44 sec.

E2.19 A microcentury is longer (it is 52.6 min).

E2.20 16,700 mile/hr.

E2.21 (1) 11,300 m/sec. (2) Mach 34 if the speed of sound is taken to be 331 m/sec (dry air at 0 °C); Mach 32.8 if the speed of sound is taken to be 344 m/sec (typical moist air at 20 °C).

E2.22 About 150,000 years.

E2.23 (1) 1.10×10^{30} electrons.
(2) About 1.8×10^{51} electrons.

E2.24 (1) 1.102 American lb/German pound; 0.907 German pound/American lb. (2) The American pound at $0.80 is a better buy.

E2.25 (1) 4.10×10^{-16} J. (2) Sample answers appear in the table below.

Mass		Speed	Time	
lb	kg	m/sec	sec	years
120	54.5	3.88×10^{-9}	2.58×10^8	8.2
150	68.1	3.47×10^{-9}	2.88×10^8	9.1
180	81.7	3.17×10^{-9}	3.16×10^8	10.0

E2.26 Ratio = $2c^2/v^2 = 5.0 \times 10^{11}$.

E2.27 (1) 6.24×10^{18} electrons. (2) Yes (I = 60 A).

E2.28 (1) $e/m_p = 9.58 \times 10^7$ C/kg = 2.87×10^{14} esu/gm.
(2) 9.58×10^4 C (or 2.87×10^{14} esu).
(3) 3.5×10^{-15} (or 1 in 2.9×10^{14}).

E2.29 For m = 15 kg, r = 1 m, and v = 3 m/sec, L ≅ 50 kg m^2/sec. Reasonable range 20 to 200.

E2.30 (a) $v \sim 1/\sqrt{r}$. (b) $L \sim \sqrt{r}$. (c) $T \sim r^{3/2}$.

E2.31 (a) Sample answers: 5' 4" = 1.626 m → 5.42×10^{-9} sec.
5' 8" = 1.727 m → 5.76×10^{-9} sec.
6' = 1.829 m → 6.10×10^{-9} sec.
(b) 5.36×10^{-6} sec. (c) 3.156×10^7 sec.

. . . .

P2.1 (1) No. (2) 1.224×10^5 kg/heft, or 8.17×10^{-6} heft/kg. Optional: K = 1.224×10^5 N sec^2/heft m.

P2.2 One line of reasoning: ρ and η contain the mass dimension, a and v do not. Therefore a dimensionless combination must contain the ratio ρ/η to be free of the mass dimension. This ratio has the dimension T/L^2, which cannot be cancelled by a or v alone but can be cancelled by the product av, whose dimension is L^2/T.

P2.3 (2) $T = K_2 v/g$. (3) Theoretical values in the absence of air resistance are $K_1 = 1$ and $K_2 = \sqrt{2} = 1.41$.

P2.4 (1) $\sqrt{\ell/g}$. (3) The theoretical period is $T = 2\pi\sqrt{\ell/g}$.

P2.5 (1) Variables m, R, r, and g. Combination with the dimension of time is

$$\left(\frac{r}{R}\right)^n \sqrt{\frac{r}{g}} ,$$

where n is an arbitrary constant. It is permissible, but somewhat less satisfactory, to include the speed v as an independent variable. Then the combination $\sqrt{r/g}$ above can be replaced by r/v.
(2) Dimensional analysis alone cannot reveal whether the period increases or decreases with increasing r, since n could be positive or negative. (In fact, $T = 2\pi(r/R)\sqrt{r/g}$; it increases with increasing r.)

P2.6 322 lb.

P2.7 Place object 1 outside the craft so that it has zero or negligible velocity relative to the craft. Then throw out object 2, whose mass is known, and measure the velocity of <u>both</u> objects relative to the craft. Object 1 provides the "stationary" reference point. (It is possible in principle to make the mass measurement by throwing both objects. Discarding only one object will not suffice.)

P2.8 (1) $\Delta K = \frac{1}{2}m(\Delta v)^2 + mv_L\Delta v$.
(2) A straight line of slope $m\Delta v$ and intercept $\Delta K_o = \frac{1}{2}m(\Delta v)^2$. Optional: Probably more hazardous at high speed. Although ΔK becomes a smaller fraction of K_L, the absolute magnitude of ΔK increases.

P2.9 (1) and (2) (a) $h/m_pc = 1.32$ fm.
(b) $h/m_pc^2 = 4.41 \times 10^{-24}$ sec.
(c) $m_pc^2 = 9.38 \times 10^8$ eV.

P2.10 (1) Mass unit = m_o, length unit = h/m_oc, time unit = h/m_oc^2. (2) Mass unit = h/ℓ_oc, length unit = ℓ_o, time unit = ℓ_o/c. (3) Yes.

CHAPTER 3

Q3.3 In terms of purposes, functions, and goals, for example, as in human organs or devices of technology; in terms of history, as in geological formations.

Q3.6 According to present usage, an alpha particle is composite, not elementary, and a beta particle is elementary.

Q3.8 The particle lost energy (and speed) in passing through the plate. The smaller radius of curvature of the track above the plate indicates a slower particle there.

Q3.10 Yes, yes, yes, and no. The oppositely charged pairs make short-lived "atoms."

Q3.11 (1) For the pion, $mc^2 \cong 140$ MeV, which is more energy than is available in an ordinary nuclear transformation. (2) This much energy can be supplied in a high-energy collision.

Q3.19 A single energetic particle may ionize millions of atoms.

Q3.20 1. The ejected electron may acquire excess kinetic energy. 2. The electron that is ejected may come from "deep" within the atom and require more than the minimum ionization energy to be freed.

. . . .

E3.1 (1) ^{60}Ni. (2) ^{234}Th.

E3.2 (2) 1.41 fm for $\pi^{\pm}$; 1.46 fm for π^0.
(3) The pion is the lightest strongly interacting particle and therefore is the exchange particle with the longest range, since m is in the denominator of $\hbar/mc$.

E3.3 $\Delta x \cong 3 \times 10^{-12}$ m; when it decays, the particle will be outside the nucleus but still well within the atom.

E3.4 (1) 3.3×10^{-14} sec, less than the lifetime of any charged particle in Table 3.1.
(2) $\Delta x \cong 10^{-13}$ m, less than the diameter of an atom.

E3.5 (1) π^0, η, Σ^0. (2) The neutron.

E3.6 (1) $p + e^- + \overline{\nu_e} + \nu_\mu + \overline{\nu_\mu} + 2\gamma$.
(2) The average charge decreases (from $+\frac{1}{2}$ for the nucleon to -1 for the omega).

E3.7 (1) (a) Negative pions curve clockwise; positive pions curve counterclockwise. (b) A slower particle leaves a more intense track. (2) It is negative. Since its radius of curvature decreases as it loses energy, it must be spiraling clockwise.

E3.9 3.3×10^4 ions (or twice that number if electrons are counted).

. . . .

P3.1 (1) For light nuclei, the electric repulsion between protons is small in its effect, so $N \cong Z$, as dictated by the strong interactions.
(2) For heavy nuclei, the electric repulsion between protons acts to diminish the binding of protons, so stable nuclei have fewer protons than neutrons.
(3) Protons are more stable (have less mass) than neutrons. This fact makes ^{3}He more stable than ^{3}H. For heavier nuclei, the electric repulsion between protons is a more important effect than the n-p mass difference.

(4) At sufficiently large Z, the electric repulsion of the many protons in the nucleus prevents the formation of any long-lived nuclei.

P3.2 Suggestion: Tell students to include no particles more massive than the neutron in their considerations. The best value of m_o is around $68m_e$. In units of $68m_e$, some particle masses are the following:

$\mu^{\pm}$:	3.04	K^0:	14.33
$\pi^{\pm}$:	4.02	η :	15.80
π^0:	3.88	p :	27.00
K^+:	14.21	n :	27.04

These numbers are closer to integers than would be expected by chance. The significance (if any) of this fact is unknown.

P3.3 Neutron mean free path $\cong$ 0.4 m (about 2×10^9 atomic diameters). A neutron must penetrate 2×10^9 atoms to encounter a total nuclear cross-sectional area of 4 $Å^2$. Answers in the range 0.1 to 1 m are acceptable. A charged particle would be expected to penetrate a lesser distance because (a) it interacts with atomic electrons and (b) it is deflected by a nucleus even if it misses the nucleus.

P3.4 Since the points do not lie exactly on an exponential curve, the extrapolated values may have a considerable range.

Energy: 10^6 to 10^7 GeV for an exponential approximation, or as little as 10^5 GeV for a non-exponential fit.

Diameter: about 1,000 to 2,000 miles.

Cost: $\$10^{12}$ to $\$10^{13}$, or as little as $\$10^{11}$ for a non-exponential fit. (For comparison, the U.S. gross national product is about $\$10^{12}$.)

CHAPTER 4

Q4.2 Examples: temperature, pressure, and density (for sufficiently slow change); speed (for a body undergoing translational motion).

Q4.4 The body is not an isolated system. Its change of charge is compensated by an opposite change of the rug's charge.

Q4.7 For example: the transformation of nuclear energy to radiant energy in the sun (creation of photons) and the transformation of solar energy to other forms of energy on earth (annihilation of photons).

Q4.10 Yes in principle, no in practice. Because of baryon conservation, this could occur only if 1 kg of anti-matter were available.

Q4.12 Not absolute. Heat may be transformed to other kinds of energy.

Q4.13 A requirement of momentum conservation.

Q4.14 In infinitely many directions, but always with the initial velocities of the fragments oppositely directed. The fragments have equal mass and must have equal magnitude of momentum; therefore they have equal kinetic energy.

Q4.15 The ball is not isolated; an external force acts on it.

Q4.16 The answer should take into account both momentum conservation and angular momentum conservation.

Q4.20 Both momentum and angular momentum would seem not to be conserved.

Q4.21 Mass, temperature, pressure, density; also acceleration if the frames are inertial frames.

Q4.22 Energy, momentum, angular momentum.

. . . .

E4.1 3.16×10^{32} electrons. 1.06×10^{6} kg.

E4.2
$$\bar{n} + p \rightarrow \bar{n} + p$$
$$\rightarrow \bar{n} + n + \pi^{+}$$
$$\rightarrow \pi^{+} + \pi^{0}$$
$$\rightarrow \pi^{+} + \pi^{+} + \pi^{-}$$
etc.

E4.3 $\mu^{+} \rightarrow e^{+} + \nu_{e} + \overline{\nu_{\mu}}$.

E4.4 $dE/dt = 0$.

E4.5 Up to 4 pions may be produced with zero total charge: π^{0}, $\pi^{+}\pi^{-}$, etc. (8 possible combinations).

E4.6 (1) MLT^{-1}. (2) kg m/sec.

E4.7 5.01×10^{-17} m/sec.

E4.8 All three answers are the same: upward out of the page.

E4.9 (1) Greater at perihelion. (2) 3.3 percent.

E4.11 $\Sigma^+ \rightarrow p + \pi^0$.

E4.12 (a) and (d) are allowed.

E4.13 (a) charge
muon-family number
(angular momentum)

(b) energy
muon-family number
(angular momentum)

(c) allowed

(d) baryon number
(angular momentum)

(e) charge

(f) electron-family number
(angular momentum)

[Note: The student need not be expected to understand the nonconservation of angular momentum in these processes.]

E4.14 (a) charge
electron-family number
muon-family number

(b) electron-family number
baryon number

(c) energy
muon-family number
(angular momentum--see note under E4.13 above)

(d) charge
electron-family number
muon-family number

. . . .

P4.1 The products must have net charge +2, net baryon number +2, and net electron-family and muon-family numbers zero.

P4.2 Examples of processes forbidden by only one conservation law:

energy: $p \rightarrow n + e^+ + \nu_e$,

charge: $e^- \rightarrow \nu_e + \gamma$,

muon-family number: $\mu^- \rightarrow e^- + \bar{\nu}_e + \bar{\nu}_\mu$,

baryon number: $p + p \rightarrow \pi^+ + \pi^+$.

P4.3 (1) (a) 67.5 MeV, 1.08×10^{-11} J. (b) 3.60×10^{-20} kg m/sec. (c) Photons are oppositely directed. (2) Energy and momentum in particular. (3) Photons need not be oppositely directed. The total energy of the photons would exceed 135 MeV and need not be equally divided.

P4.4 (2) Momentum: $\mathbf{p}_1 + \mathbf{p}_2$ defines a plane; since $\mathbf{p}_1 + \mathbf{p}_2 + \mathbf{p}_3 = 0$, $\mathbf{p}_3$ must lie in that plane.

P4.5 The conservation laws are

$$m_1v_1 = m_2v_2 ,$$

$$\tfrac{1}{2}m_1v_1^2 + m_1c^2 = \tfrac{1}{2}m_2v_2^2 + m_2c^2 .$$

These lead to the equations $v_1 = \sqrt{2m_2/m_1}\, c$ and $v_2 = \sqrt{2m_1/m_2}\, c$. There is no ratio m_1/m_2 that permits both $v_1 < c$ and $v_2 < c$.

P4.6 The conservation laws for the special case are

$$mv_0 = mv_1 + mv_2 ,$$

$$\tfrac{1}{2}mv_0^2 + mc^2 = \tfrac{1}{2}mv_1^2 + \tfrac{1}{2}mv_2^2 + 2mc^2 .$$

These lead to the equation $v_1(v_0 - v_1) = v_1v_2 = c^2$, which does not permit both v_1 and v_2 to be less than c.

P4.7 (1) Let the set E contain N_E guests who have shaken hands an even (or zero) number of times; let the set O contain N_O guests who have shaken hands an odd number of times. Whenever two members of the same set shake hands, they move to the other set; then both N_E and N_O change by 2.
(2) The "parity" of N_O is conserved. It is even. [The parity of N_E is also conserved. It is even if the total number of guests is even and odd if the total number of guests is odd.]

CHAPTER 5

Q5.6 Trigonometry (although it may not deserve the name "discipline"), probability and statistics, group theory, celestial mechanics, perhaps calculus.

Q5.8 Both. [The explanation of the outer truth is not trivial. (The instructor might mention the relativistic law of velocity addition.)]

Q5.14 (1) No. (2) Yes.

Q5.15 (1) Yes. (2) No.

Q5.16 (1) Yes. (2) Yes.

Q5.17 Time is the independent variable; number of people is the dependent variable. They can be interchanged.

Q5.18 m^2/sec (or any other area/time unit).

Q5.19 Pressure or potential, for example. Velocity, for example.

Q5.21 Statics, for example (force and distance).

Q5.23 (1) 4. (2) 2.

Q5.24

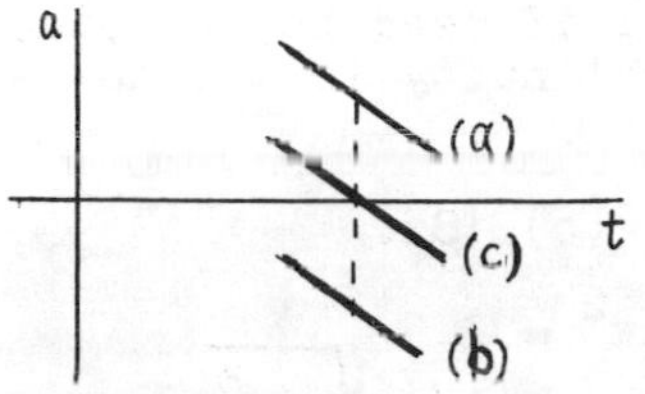

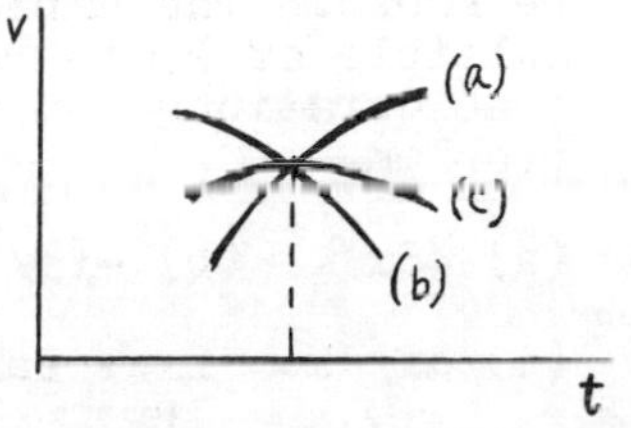

(1) The acceleration is decreasing. (It could be (a) positive, (b) negative, or (c) momentarily zero.)

(2) The given information is insufficient to know. (The speed could be (a) increasing, (b) decreasing, or (c) momentarily not changing.)

Q5.26 It is his total earnings in the time span a to b. It is measured in dollars (or other currency).

Q5.28 Velocity. (More exactly, it is the component of velocity along the arc, or approximately the horizontal component.)

Q5.29 Almost any example of oscillatory motion. Also linear components of uniform circular motion.

Q5.30 Total number of radioactive disintegrations in a given time span.

Q5.31 About 7×10^9.

Q5.34 The uncertainties may have been overestimated.

. . . .

E5.1 (1)

	+1	−1	i	−i
+1	1	−1	i	−i
−1	−1	1	−i	i
i	i	−i	−1	1
−i	−i	i	1	−1

(2) i.

E5.2 (2) Rotating about a fixed axis through 0 deg, 120 deg, and 240 deg, for example. Rotating through 180 deg about any of three mutually perpendicular axes, for example.

E5.4 (1) $x^2 + y^2 = a^2$. (2) $r = a$.

E5.5 (2) The coordinate r is defined to be positive; the positive square root must be taken. The ratio y/x determines two physically distinct angles. To specify the quadrant, the sign of y or x must also be known. The ambiguity of θ to within an additive multiple of 2π is resolved, if need be, by other considerations, such as continuity in a time-varying problem.

E5.6 (a) $48x^3$. (b) $-(3/2)x^{-3}$. (c) $18x$.

E5.7 (1) $df/dx = 2x + 2a$, $d^2f/dx^2 = 2$.

(2) $dg/dy = \frac{1}{2}\sqrt{a/y}$, $d^2g/dy^2 = -(1/4)\sqrt{a/y^3}$.

(3) $dh/dz = -2ze^{-z^2}$, $d^2h/dz^2 = (-2 + 4z^2)e^{-z^2}$.

(4) $dx/dt = A\omega \cos \omega t - B\omega \sin \omega t$, $d^2x/dt^2 = -A\omega^2 \sin \omega t - B\omega^2 \cos \omega t$.

E5.8 Zero.

E5.10 (2) $dx/dt = at$; $dt/dx = 1/\sqrt{2ax} = 1/at$.

E5.11 (2) The slope of the trajectory in the xy plane (or $\tan \theta$, where θ is the angle between the velocity vector and the x axis).

E5.15 9.549 rpm/(radian/sec), or 0.1047 (radian/sec)/rpm.

E5.16 (1) (c)(b)(e)(a)(f)(d). (2) (a) 1.75×10^{-3}, (b) 1.45×10^{-4}, (c) 1.99×10^{-7}, (d) 88.0, (e) 1.16×10^{-3}, (f) 62.8, all in radian/sec.

E5.17 168 m/sec, about half the speed of sound.

E5.18 (a) 0. (b) 0. (c) −0.707. (d) 1. (e) −1.

E5.19 (1) $L_x = 3.464$ units, $L_y = 2.00$ units.

(2) $L_x^2 + L_y^2 = L^2$.

E5.24 (2) $dV/d\ell = 3\ell^2$. It is the rate of change of the cube's volume with respect to the length of one side. Its dimension is L^2.

E5.25 (1) $\bar{v} = C\sqrt{T}$. (2) Note infinite slope at T = 0. (3) Note infinite value at T = 0.

E5.26 (1) 0.25 m/sec. (2) 1 m/sec. (3) The particle received a sudden impulse that changed its velocity instantaneously. A true discontinuity of velocity would require infinite force, which cannot be realized in nature.

E5.27 (1) A straight line through the origin with slope 2A. (2) $(\text{temperature})/(\text{length})^2$.

E5.28 (2) An initially heated ball in a cooler environment. (3) A straight line through the origin with negative slope 2A.

E5.29 (1) $v_0 = 1.5$ m/sec. (2) $x_0 = 2.0$ m. (3) At x = 17 m.

E5.31 (a) a_0/v. (b) $a_0/\sqrt{v_0^2 + 2a_0(x - x_0)}$. (c) $a_0/(v_0 + a_0 t)$.

E5.32 (1) Successive (t,x) values joined by straight lines: (0,0), (2,6), (4,6), (6,10), (8,0). (2) Horizontal line segments, each of length 2 sec, at $v_x = +3, 0, +2$, and -5. (3) Infinite.

E5.33 (1) Acceleration falls from an initial value of about 10 m/sec^2 to zero in about 3 sec, then goes to a small negative value, then to a small positive value, and then back to zero. (2) $\bar{v} \cong 8.6$ m/sec (range 8 to 9 acceptable).

E5.34 (1) 1 m/sec. (2) 5×10^4 m/sec^2. (3) 2×10^{-5} sec. (These answers use g = 10 m/sec^2.)

E5.35 (1) $s = 2t - 1.5t^2$, $v = 2 - 3t$ (mks units). (2) 0.667 m. (3) At t = 1.333 sec.

E5.36 (2) $K_f = K_0 + mgh$. The graph is a straight line of unit slope that intercepts the K_f axis at mgh.

E5.37 (1) $v = 3Et^2$, $a = 6Et$. (2) A reasonable value of E is around 0.1 m/sec^3. (In 3 sec, the elevator would then rise 2.7 m and reach a speed of 2.7 m/sec and an acceleration of 0.18g.)

E5.38 (1) At small t, the graph rises parabolically ($x \cong \frac{1}{2}at^2$); at large t, x approaches a constant ($x \to \frac{1}{2}at_0^2$). (2) a (dimension LT^{-2}) is the initial acceleration; t_0 (dimension T) is the time required for x to reach half its final value.

E5.39 (1) $x^4 + x^5 + C$. (2) $(2/3)\sqrt{ay^3} + C$.
(3) $-(A/\omega)\cos\omega t + (B/\omega)\sin\omega t + C$.
(4) $\theta \ln k\theta + C$.

E5.40 (Use $v = \int a\,dt$ and $x = \int v\,dt$.)

E5.41 (1) $\theta = \int \omega\,dt$. (2) $\theta = \theta_0 + \omega t$.
(3) $\theta = \theta_0 + \omega_0 t + \frac{1}{2}\alpha t^2$.

E5.42 (Integrate $\int (dT/dx)\,dx$ to get $T = Ax + (1/3)Bx^3 + C$ and adjust C to fit the boundary condition.)

E5.43 (1) 20. (2) 2/3. (3) 0. (4) 0.

E5.44 (1) $v(t_1) - v(0)$, which is $v(t_1)$. (2) Zero.
(3) The net displacement, $x(\infty) - x(0) = x(\infty)$.

E5.45 $w\int_0^L d(x)\,dx$, a definite integral.

E5.46 (1) 1.59 Hz. (2) 0.628 sec. (3) 0.3 m/sec.

E5.47 [Suggestion for an optional extension of this exercise: Show that the infinite series for sin x and cos x in Appendix 6 (page A22) satisfy Equations 5.92 and 5.94.]

E5.49 (2) λ = wavelength, $\omega = 2\pi\nu$ = angular frequency.
(3) $x = \frac{1}{2}n\lambda$, where n is a positive or negative integer or zero.

E5.50 (1) $-\cos(1/x)/x^2$. (2) It has an infinite number of oscillations between an arbitrarily small finite x and zero.

E5.51 $n = 20$. Amount of money is $N = 2^n$.

E5.53 5.48×10^{-7} sec.

E5.54 1855.

E5.55 (a) $E = E_0 e^{(t - 1932)/\tau_1}$, with $E_0 \cong 3$ MeV and $\tau_1 \cong 3.2$ years; doubling time about 2.2 years.
(b) $d = d_0 e^{(t - 1932)/\tau_2}$, with $d_0 \cong 0.8$ ft and $\tau_2 \cong 4.2$ years; doubling time about 2.9 years.

E5.57 (2) $z = A\sin x + B\cos x$.

E5.60 (1) Length. (2) No, for there $s = -\infty$ and $v = +\infty$.
(3) a/t_0. (4) No, although $v \to 0$ as $t \to \infty$.

E5.61 Fractional uncertainty $1/\sqrt{n}$. Fourfold increase in n.

E5.62 (1) ±7 Å (answers in the range ±5 to ±11 Å are acceptable). (2) Yes. (There appears to be a systematic error of about -7 Å.)

. . . .

P5.3 In the moving frame, the particle's only energy is its rest energy mc^2, which must equal the total energy of the product particles.

P5.4 (1) $x = r \sin\theta \cos\varphi$, $y = r \sin\theta \sin\varphi$, $z = r \cos\theta$. (2) (Consider infinitesimal displacements that result when two of the three coordinates are held fixed and the third varies.)

P5.6 (Depending on how the limit in Equation 5.6 is taken, the derivative at t = 4 could have any value from 0.25 m/sec to 1 m/sec.)

P5.7 (3) At 35 cm, about 1.3 kg (reasonable range 1.2 to 1.5 kg). At 175 cm, about 61 kg (reasonable range 58 to 66 kg).

P5.8 (2) The motion is apparently uniformly accelerated for 4 sec and then carried out at constant speed for the next 4 sec. (This is not absolutely certain, since s is specified only at certain times.) (3) 20 m/sec. (4) No. (But simple functions suffice in separate ranges: from t = 0 to 4 sec, $s = 2.5t^2$; from t = 4 to 8 sec, s = -40 + 20t.)

P5.9 (1) Yes. (2) $T_0 = 251.0 \pm 0.1$ K, $A = 0.900 \pm 0.003$ K/cm^2.

P5.10 (1) About 1 percent. (2)

It is consistent to assume a constant ratio.

Trial	v_C/v_B
1	1.411
2	1.426
3	1.392
4	1.431

(3) n = 0.50.

P5.11 With x measured downward and the origin placed at the point where v = 0, the equation is $v = \alpha x$ (or $dx/dt = \alpha x$). Its solution is $x = x_0 e^{\alpha(t - t_0)}$; velocity and acceleration also increase exponentially. To move downward, an object must be thrown downward. The only solution with $v_0 = 0$ is x = 0: an object released at rest remains at rest. (The same conclusion can be reached by examining the acceleration, $a = \alpha^2 x$; if $x_0 = v_0 = 0$, $a = 0$ and there is no motion.) Similar difficulties result if one starts with $v = v_0 + \alpha x$ or its equivalent, $v = \alpha(x - x_0)$. [Note that these equations lack time-reversal invariance. They imply that an upward-thrown ball also gains speed. If the sign of α is reversed for an upward-thrown ball, the ball slows but needs an infinite time to reach its maximum height.]

P5.12 (2) v vs t.

P5.13 (1) $a_x = -5$ m/sec^2. (2) $v_x = -10$ m/sec. (3) No. (4) 10 m.

P5.14 (1) 1.581 (or the inverse, 0.632).
(2) 2.50 (or the inverse, 0.400). [The required initial speeds are 8.85 m/sec and 14.0 m/sec.]

P5.15 (2) 50 m. (3) $v_x(t) = 15 - 3t + 0.15t^2$,

$x(t) = 15t - 1.5t^2 + 0.05t^3$ (in mks units).

P5.16 (1) $x = x_0 + At + A\tau(e^{-t/\tau} - 1)$

$= x_0 + 67t - 402(1 - e^{-t/6})$ in mks units.

$a = (A/\tau)e^{-t/\tau} = 11.18e^{-t/6}$ in mks units.

(3) $x \cong x_0 + \frac{1}{2}At^2/\tau$, $v \cong At/\tau$, $a \cong A/\tau$.

P5.17 (1) (a) $\bar{v} = v$. (b) $\bar{v} = v_0 + \frac{1}{2}aT$.

P5.18 (1) (It is an ellipse.) (2) $v_x = -a\omega \sin\omega t$,

$v_y = b\omega \cos\omega t$, $v = \omega\sqrt{a^2 \sin^2\omega t + b^2 \cos^2\omega t}$.
The speed is maximum where the orbit is closest to the origin (e.g. at $x = 0$, $y = \pm b$ if $a > b$) and minimum where the orbit is farthest from the origin.
(3) $dy/dx = -(b/a) \text{ ctn } \omega t = -(b/a)^2(x/y)$. The slope is zero at $x = 0$, $y = \pm b$, and infinite at $x = \pm a$, $y = 0$. The infinite slope is not unphysical.

P5.20 $\delta A = \frac{1}{2}[f(x + \Delta x) - f(x)]\Delta x \cong \frac{1}{2}(df/dx)(\Delta x)^2$.
$\delta A/\Delta A = \frac{1}{2}[f(x + \Delta x) - f(x)]/f(x) \to 0$ as $\Delta x \to 0$.

P5.21 (1) $\bar{\lambda} = 5{,}885$ Å. (2) $\Delta\lambda = 6.78$ Å.
Optional: $\bar{\lambda} = 5{,}885 \pm 2.8$ Å (if systematic error is ignored).

P5.22 Acceptable range of answers ± 8 cm/sec to ± 30 cm/sec. [A least-squares fit requiring that the line pass through the origin gives $x = (304 \pm 10$ cm/sec$)t$. A least-squares fit that does not require the line to pass through the origin gives $dx/dt = 317 \pm 24$ cm/sec.]

CHAPTER 6

Q6.1 Numerical: (b), (d), (h). Vector: (a), (c), (g). Other: (e), (f).

Q6.2 Scalar: (b), (c), (d). Numerical but not scalar: (a), (e).

Q6.3 No.

Q6.5 They must be equal in magnitude (and unit of measurement, if any) and opposite in direction.

Q6.6 $C_{max} = 2A = 2B$. $C_{min} = 0$.

Q6.8 No. No.

Q6.9 (a), (b), (c), (d).

Q6.10 Yes; a requirement of momentum conservation. Yes, two or more neutral particles may have been produced.

Q6.12 The results are the same, a zero vector.

Q6.13 They would be oppositely directed.

Q6.14 (1) Yes. (2) No.

Q6.15 (1) Changes in both magnitude and direction.
(2) Changes in both magnitude and direction.

Q6.18 A position vector.

Q6.19 (1) Components change. Magnitude does not change. (Also the direction of the vector in "space"--i.e., its direction relative to other vectors or to physical objects--does not change.) (2) No aspect of a scalar is changed.

Q6.20 A component of a vector, for example.

Q6.22 No. Since different forms of energy can be added (a requirement of energy conservation), all must be scalar if one is scalar.

Q6.23 (Such an equation, if correct in one coordinate system, would be incorrect in another.)

Q6.24 Axial vector quantity.

Q6.25 An axial vector.

Q6.26 A true scalar.

Q6.27 While the car is moving to the rear, $\mathbf{a}$ is directed first to the rear, then forward. While the car is moving forward, $\mathbf{a}$ is directed first forward, then to the left.

Q6.29 Tangent to the circle, opposite to the velocity.

Q6.30 The rate of turning (angular speed) of $\mathbf{v}$ is doubled, which would double the rate of change of a vector of fixed magnitude. The magnitude of $\mathbf{v}$ is doubled, which would double its rate of change at a constant angular speed. Each of these factors of 2 is at work, producing a 4-fold increase in the rate of change of $\mathbf{v}$.

Q6.31 The magnitude of $\mathbf{v}$ is unchanged. Its rate of turning (angular speed) is halved, which halves its rate of change.

. . . .

E6.2 The third force is directed 60 deg south of west (or 30 deg west of south) and has magnitude 6.0 N.

E6.3 (1) (a) 2. (b) 0. (c) 1.414.
(2) One must be rotated 120 deg from the other.

E6.4 $\Delta\mathbf{v}$ is directed to the southeast (45 deg south of east) and has a magnitude of 14.14 m/sec.

E6.5 (1) 30 deg west of north. (2) 86.6 mile/hr.

E6.6 240 mile/hr (directed approximately 28 deg north of east).

E6.7 He sees it coming from 26.6 deg west of north at a speed of 22.4 m/sec.

E6.8 $\leqslant$.

E6.10 $10(\mathbf{b} - \mathbf{a})$.

E6.11 (1) A vector of magnitude 13 m directed 22.6 deg south of east; its eastward component is 12 m and its southward component is 5 m. (2) The same as his final position vector.

E6.13 (1) $\mathbf{r}_1 = \mathbf{R} + \mathbf{r}_1'$ and $\mathbf{r}_2 = \mathbf{R} + \mathbf{r}_2'$, where $\mathbf{R}$ is the displacement vector from O to O'.

E6.14 (a) A vector of magnitude 14.14 cm directed from 3 to 6 on the clock face (45 deg to the vertical). (b) A vector of magnitude 20 cm directed vertically upward from 6 to 12 on the clock face. (c) Zero.

E6.15 (1) $A_x = A_y = 1.994$ (approximately 2.00). $B_x = 1.732$, $B_y = 1.00$. (2) Sum $\mathbf{S} = \mathbf{A} + \mathbf{B}$: magnitude, 4.78; direction, 38.8 deg counterclockwise from the x axis; components, $S_x = 3.73$, $S_y = 2.99$ (approximately 3.00). (3) Difference $\mathbf{T} = \mathbf{A} - \mathbf{B}$: magnitude, 1.03; direction, 75.2 deg counterclockwise from the x axis; components, $T_x = 0.26$, $T_y = 0.99$ (approximately 1.00).

E6.16 (2) $C_x = 9.18$, $C_y = 6.99$ ($\mathbf{C}$ is in the first quadrant at an angle of 37.3 deg to the x axis; its magnitude is 11.54). $D_x = 7.93$, $D_y = 5.00$ ($\mathbf{D}$ is in the first quadrant at an angle of 32.2 deg to the x axis; its magnitude is 9.37). (3) No (unless $\alpha = \beta = 0$ is admitted).

E6.17 (1) $F_{1x} = 10$, $F_{1y} = 0$; $F_{2x} = 0$, $F_{2y} = 10$; $F_{3x} = 7.07$, $F_{3y} = 7.07$. (2) $F_x = 17.07$, $F_y = 17.07$. (3) Magnitude 24.1, direction northeast.

E6.18 $v_x = 212$ mile/hr, $v_y = 112$ mile/hr. (See also E6.6.)

E6.19 (1) Equal vectors: none. Equal magnitudes: A = B and C = E. Same direction: $\mathbf{A}$ and $\mathbf{D}$. Opposite direction: $\mathbf{B}$ and $\mathbf{E}$. (2) Sum $\mathbf{S} = 8\mathbf{i} + 5\mathbf{j} - 8\mathbf{k}$.

E6.20 $x = r \cos \alpha$, $y = r \sin \alpha$.

E6.21 (1) Slightly less. (2) Slightly less.

E6.23 (a) 1,061 N m. (b) 1,061 N m. (c) 321 N m.

E6.24 $\mathbf{i} \cdot \mathbf{i}' = \mathbf{j} \cdot \mathbf{i}' = \mathbf{j} \cdot \mathbf{j}' = 0.707$; $\mathbf{i} \cdot \mathbf{j}' = -0.707$.

E6.26 (a) 0. (b) -9. (c) -16.

E6.27 (a) $12\mathbf{k}$ (upward out of the page). (b) $12\mathbf{k}$. (c) $12\mathbf{k}$. (d) $-12\mathbf{k}$.

E6.28 (a) 0. (b) $-48\mathbf{j}$ (direction opposite to $\mathbf{B}$). (c) $36\mathbf{i} - 48\mathbf{j}$ (downward to the right in the page, perpendicular to $\mathbf{C}$; magnitude 60).

E6.29 $\mathbf{A} \cdot \mathbf{B} = 5.45$. $\mathbf{A} \times \mathbf{B} = -1.46\mathbf{k}$ (into the page).

E6.30 (1) (a) 0. (b) 0. (c) $\mathbf{k}$. (d) $-\mathbf{j}$. (e) $\mathbf{j}$. (2) Let the first axis have the direction of $\mathbf{i}_1$ and let the second axis have the direction of $\mathbf{i}_2$, with $\mathbf{i}_1 \cdot \mathbf{i}_2 = 0$. The third axis should have the direction of $\mathbf{i}_1 \times \mathbf{i}_2$.

E6.31 (a) 0. (b) $-\mathbf{j}$. (c) 0. (d) 1. (e) 0.

E6.32 (1) $r = 6$ m, $v = 5.83$ m/sec. (2) 59.04 deg. (3) $\mathbf{r} \cdot \mathbf{v} = 18$ m^2/sec, $\mathbf{r} \times \mathbf{v} = 30\mathbf{k}$ m^2/sec.

E6.33 (1) $\mathbf{r}(0) = 3.4\mathbf{i}$ (on the x axis 3.4 from the origin). (2) At $t = 1$ sec. (3) At $t = 0.5$ sec; then $\mathbf{r} = 3.4\mathbf{i} + 2.75\mathbf{j} + 1.225\mathbf{k}$.

E6.34 (1) $\mathbf{r} = x_1\mathbf{i} + y_1\mathbf{j} + (z_0 + v_0t - \frac{1}{2}gt^2)\mathbf{k}$. (2) $\mathbf{v} = (v_0 - gt)\mathbf{k}$. (3) $\mathbf{a} = -g\mathbf{k}$.

E6.35 (2) Motion with variable speed in a circle, for example, or possibly any orbital motion.

E6.36 (1) $\mathbf{r} = 3 \cos 2t\ \mathbf{i} + 3 \sin 2t\ \mathbf{j}$. (2) $\mathbf{v} = -6 \sin 2t\ \mathbf{i} + 6 \cos 2t\ \mathbf{j}$. (Both answers assume mks units.)

E6.37 8 m/sec^2. Yes, a transverse acceleration of 0.8g is reasonable for a racing car.

E6.38 (1) 2.42 m/sec^2, about $\frac{1}{4}$g. (2) Altitude = 3,950 miles (approximately Earth's radius); period = 240 min.

E6.39 1,020 m, or 0.634 mile. <u>Optional</u>: 45 deg.

E6.40 By itself, the vanishing of $\mathbf{a} \cdot \mathbf{v}$ does not prove that $\mathbf{a}$ is directed toward the center; it could also be directed away from the center.

E6.42 $\mathbf{r} = r \cos \frac{1}{2}\alpha t^2\ \mathbf{i} + r \sin \frac{1}{2}\alpha t^2\ \mathbf{j}$,
$\mathbf{v} = r\alpha t(-\sin \frac{1}{2}\alpha t^2\ \mathbf{i} + \cos \frac{1}{2}\alpha t^2\ \mathbf{j})$.

E6.43 (1) $d\mathbf{p}/dt = m(d\mathbf{v}/dt) + (dm/dt)\mathbf{v}$. (2) $\mathbf{a} = -(dm/dt)\mathbf{v}/m = -[d(\ln m)/dt]\mathbf{v}$. The acceleration has the same direction as the velocity if the rocket mass is decreasing.

. . . .

P6.2 (1) Partly upstream, at an angle of 60 deg to the bank (or 30 deg to the desired course). (2) Perpendicular to the bank. (3) 0.866 mile/hr in the first case, 1.118 mile/hr in the second case. (4) 1 mile/hr in both cases.

P6.3 In the plane of the paper at 30 deg to the π^+ track and 90 deg to the K^+ track.

P6.5 (1) 7.50 m/sec. (2) 6.50 m/sec.

P6.6 3.33 m/sec at an angle of 53.1 deg above the horizontal.

P6.9 The physical assumption is that the vector $\mathbf{F}$ is not altered in magnitude or direction by the rotation of coordinates.

P6.10 $x_1' = x_1 - X$, $y_1' = y_1 - Y$, where X and Y are the components of $\mathbf{R}$ in either of the two frames.

P6.11 (1) The unit vectors $\mathbf{i}$ and $\mathbf{i}'$ have the same direction because the x and x' axes are parallel, and they have the same magnitude (unity) by definition; therefore $\mathbf{i} = \mathbf{i}'$. The same reasoning applies to $\mathbf{j}$ and $\mathbf{j}'$. (3) At t = 0, the origin of frame S is located at x' = a. (4) The equations are valid for all points at every instant.

P6.12 (Since $\mathbf{a}$ has magnitude cos θ and the direction of $\mathbf{i}_r$, it is equal to $\mathbf{i}_r \cos\theta$; similarly, $\mathbf{b} = -\mathbf{i}_\theta \times \sin\theta$. The first of the two equations to be proved is equivalent to $\mathbf{a} + \mathbf{b} = \mathbf{i}$. A similar construction for $\mathbf{c} + \mathbf{d} = \mathbf{j}$ leads to the second equation.)

P6.14 Also needed are properties of $\alpha\mathbf{a}$: that it is a vector parallel to $\mathbf{a}$ of magnitude αa.

P6.15 The proof shows that $a_x b_x + a_y b_y$ is indeed a scalar quantity, independent of the orientation of the axes.

P6.17 (Most simply, write $a_x b_y - a_y b_x = ab(\cos\theta \sin\varphi - \sin\theta\cos\varphi) = ab\sin(\varphi - \theta) = -ab\sin(\theta - \varphi)$.)

P6.19 (2) The <u>magnitude</u> of the vector $\mathbf{a} \times \mathbf{b}$ is a scalar: it is unaffected by a rotation of coordinate axes.

P6.20 (1) $\mathbf{r} = x_1\mathbf{i} + \mathbf{v}t = (x_1 + vt\cos\theta)\mathbf{i} + vt\sin\theta\,\mathbf{j}$, where $\theta = \arctan(-y_1/x_1)$ (note that x_1 is negative). (3) Place the origin of the new system at $x = x_1$, $y = 0$ and let its x' axis be parallel to $\mathbf{v}$. Then $\mathbf{r} = \mathbf{v}t = vt\mathbf{i}'$ and $\mathbf{v} = v\mathbf{i}'$.

P6.21 (1) $\underset{\sim}{v} = v_o\underset{\sim}{i} + a_o b e^{bt}\underset{\sim}{j}$, $v = \sqrt{v_o^2 + a_o^2 b^2 e^{2bt}}$.

(2) $\underset{\sim}{a} = a_o b^2 e^{bt}\underset{\sim}{j} = b^2 y\underset{\sim}{j}$. (3) The trajectory is an exponential function: $y = a_o e^{(b/v_o)x}$.

P6.22 (1) $\underset{\sim}{r} = \frac{1}{\sqrt{2}}(v_o t + \frac{1}{2}a_o t^2)\underset{\sim}{i} + \frac{1}{\sqrt{2}}(v_o t - \frac{1}{2}a_o t^2)\underset{\sim}{j}$,

$\underset{\sim}{v} = \frac{1}{\sqrt{2}}(v_o + a_o t)\underset{\sim}{i} + \frac{1}{\sqrt{2}}(v_o - a_o t)\underset{\sim}{j}$.

(2) It is a parabola with its axis inclined at 45 deg to the x and y axes. At point O, $dy/dx = +1$. At A, $y = -4v_o^2/a_o$ and $dy/dx = -3$. At B, $x = +4v_o^2/a_o$ and $dy/dx = -1/3$.

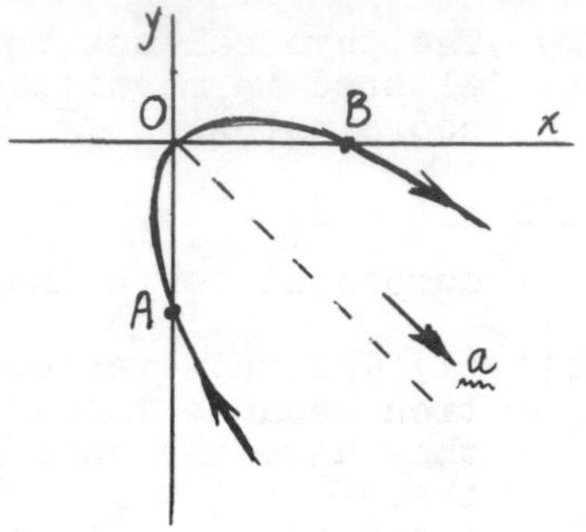

P6.23 Equation 6.90 leads to $\varphi = \pm(\frac{1}{2}\pi + \omega t)$; Equation 6.91 leads to $\varphi = \frac{1}{2}\pi \pm \omega t$. Together they imply $\varphi = \frac{1}{2}\pi + \omega t = \theta + \frac{1}{2}\pi$ (see Figure 6.37).

P6.24 The isosceles triangle formed by $\underset{\sim}{v}(t)$, $\Delta\underset{\sim}{v}$, and $\underset{\sim}{v}(t + \Delta t)$ is similar to the one in the diagram, and has the property $|\Delta\underset{\sim}{v}| = 2v\sin(\Delta\theta/2)$. Divide this expression by $\Delta t = r\Delta\theta/v$ to get $|\underset{\sim}{a}|$. In the limit of small $\Delta\theta$, the ratio is v^2/r.

P6.25 (1) $\underset{\sim}{v} = -a\omega\sin\omega t\,\underset{\sim}{i} + b\omega\cos\omega t\,\underset{\sim}{j}$, $\underset{\sim}{a} = -a\omega^2\cos\omega t\,\underset{\sim}{i} - b\omega^2\sin\omega t\,\underset{\sim}{j}$. (2) Opposite to $\underset{\sim}{r}$; $a = \omega^2 r$.

(3) $\frac{x^2}{a^2} + \frac{y^2}{b^2} = 1$.

P6.28 (2) $D_i = \int_a^b F_i(x)\,dx$.

P6.29 The x and y components of a 2-dimensional vector correspond, respectively, to the real and imaginary parts of a complex number. (a) Addition, a + b (a and b are complex numbers). (b) Subtraction, a − b. (c) Real part of a*b, or $\frac{1}{2}(a^*b + ab^*)$.

(d) Imaginary part of a*b, or $\frac{1}{2i}(a^*b - ab^*)$.

CHAPTER 7

Q7.1 Magnitude constant. Direction constant.

Q7.3 At least one. Possibly any number.

Q7.4 (1) No. Some impractical tests: Turn on a large fan nearby; move the earth. (2) Yes. Alter the motion of the nearest star or galaxy (in principle) and observe that the effect on the photon is negligible.

Q7.5 (1) By observing the motion of a puck on a frictionless air table, for example. (2) Yes, on a table rotating at 2π radian/day.

Q7.8 For example: Adjust some third variable force until its effect alone is the same as the effect of the force F alone. Then combine these two in the same direction and see if the spring extension is twice that produced by F alone.

Q7.9 In all three cases, the external forces supplied by gravity, the road, and air resistance sum to zero, but the relative magnitudes differ.

Q7.10 (1) Yes. (2) Yes. (3) (a) No. (b) No.

Q7.11 No. No.

Q7.12 At both times, the upward force of air resistance equals his weight. The net force does not change; it is zero at both times.

Q7.13 (a) Speed increasing in straight-line motion (forward or backward). (b) Speed decreasing in straight-line motion. (c) Turning at constant speed. (d) Straight-line motion at constant speed. (e) At the instant of starting or stopping. In each case, the net force is parallel to $\mathbf{a}$.

Q7.14 Yes, by a factor of 9.

Q7.17 Zeal = 1/m. No, zeals are not additive.

Q7.20 The force is position-dependent, the same at a given spring extension independent of the time at which this occurs, the speed, or other variables.

Q7.23 Double its amplitude, or decrease its mass by a factor of 4, or increase its force constant by a factor of 4. (There are infinitely many other possibilities involving simultaneous change of 2 or 3 of these variables.)

Q7.24 Weigh an object that is being horizontally accelerated, for example. Or argue that since a constant horizontal force is found to produce a constant horizontal acceleration, the constant acceleration observed in free fall demonstrates a constant vertical force (constant weight).

Q7.25 He could, for example, use a spring balance that reads in newtons (or other force units) to weigh an object of known mass; then $g_{moon} = F/m$.

Q7.30 (a) It will not keep time at all (rate = 0).
(b) It will run slow by a factor of $\sqrt{6}$ (ticking off 24.5 min per hour). Yes, it would be risky.

Q7.32 (1) Yes. (2) No. (3) No.

Q7.33 (1) Yes. (2) Yes. (3) No.

Q7.35 Yes. No.

Q7.36 6.37×10^6 m, or 3,960 miles (radius of earth).

Q7.37 Greater.

Q7.38 Less than 45 deg. [The student can be encouraged to think in the hypothetical limit of very great air resistance.]

Q7.39 A TV tube, for example, uses both.

Q7.40 Those headed straight down over a pole are undeflected and are more likely to reach the earth. (Cosmic ray flux at the surface is greater at higher latitude.)

Q7.42 No. There would be a "stationary" preferred frame of reference. The law $\underset{\sim}{F} = m\underset{\sim}{v}$ would not be true in other frames moving uniformly with respect to the preferred frame.

Q7.43 Yes, absolute velocity would have meaning. Yes, infinite acceleration would be possible in principle (just as $d^3\underset{\sim}{r}/dt^3 = 0$ is possible in principle in our world--at the moment a body is dropped from rest, for instance).

Q7.44 Yes, a uniformly accelerated frame would be an inertial frame.

Q7.45 The plane of the swinging pendulum remains fixed in an inertial frame.

. . . .

E7.1 The road exerts on the tires an upward force of 15,000 N and a forward force of 1,000 N (sum is a force of 15,033 N directed at 3.8 deg to the vertical).

E7.2 (a) 10,000 to 20,000 N. (b) ~30 to 100 N. (c) 10 to 50 N. (d) ~20 to 50 N.

E7.3 (1) 7 N, directed vertically upward. (2) The same.

E7.4 The line outperformed its guarantee by a factor of 2.

E7.5 10^5 kg.

E7.6 116.9 N.

E7.7 (1) The pan with the two lighter objects.
(2) 0.923 m/sec^2.

E7.8 (1) 6 kg. (2) Less.

E7.9 3.2×10^5 N.

E7.10

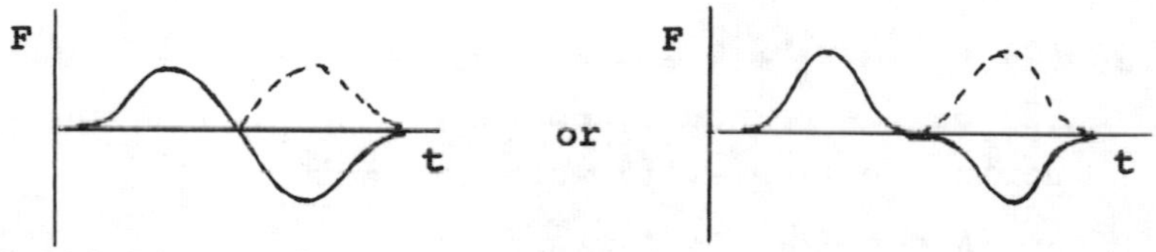

Solid line: forward component. Dashed line: magnitude. (Note that the areas under the two humps in either graph are equal.)

E7.11 20 N. [This is the net force including gravity. A common wrong answer may be 118 N, which is the non-gravitational force supplied by the other links.]

E7.12 (1) 0.612 kg. (2) 0.904 sec. (3) 4.43 m/sec.

E7.13 21.5 deg.

E7.14 $F_{Wx} = -6.52 \times 10^3$ N, $F_{Wy} = -2.74 \times 10^3$ N ($\underset{\sim}{F}_W$ is the force exerted by the water).

E7.15 12,900 N. [The net force including gravity is 8,000 N.]

E7.16 $F_{top} = F_{bottom} = m\omega^2 r$. The total force is the same because the acceleration is the same.

E7.17 (1) (a) $x = v_0 t - \frac{1}{2}(F/m)t^2$. (b) $\frac{1}{2}(mv_0^2/F)$.
(c) $2mv_0/F$. (2) (a) $x = v_0 t - \frac{1}{2}(F/m)t^2$, with $v_o < 0$.

(b) $\frac{1}{2}(mv_0{}^2/F)$ (was reached at $t = mv_0/F < 0$).
(c) Never again (was at origin at $t = 2mv_0/F < 0$).
(3)

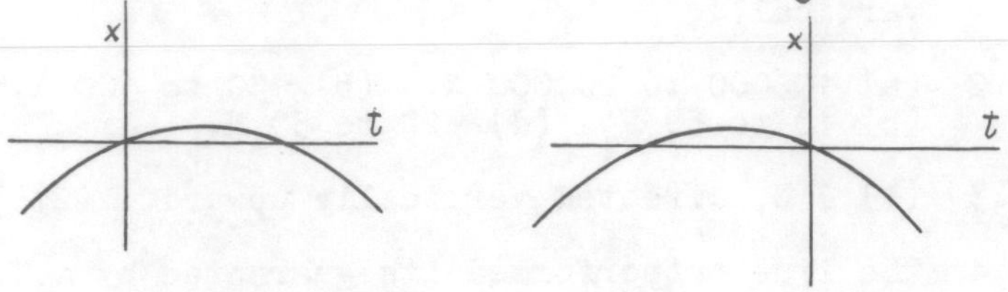

E7.18 $v = (A/mb)(1 - e^{-bt})$.

E7.19 $x = x_0 + v_0 t + \frac{1}{2}(A/m)t^2 - (\alpha/6m)t^3$.

E7.20 (1) Upward. (2) 0.2g, or 1.96 m/sec^2.

E7.21 1/3 kg.

E7.22 25 m.

E7.24 (1) $0.866A\omega$, or $0.866v_{max}$. (2) $\pm 0.866A$.

E7.25 (2) $F_x' = F_x + W = -kx + mg = -k(x - x_0)$.
(3) Simple harmonic, centered at x_0, with the same period as if gravity were not acting.

E7.26 $a = A \cos \varphi$, $b = A \sin \varphi$.

E7.27 (1) $A = B$, $\varphi = -\pi/2$ (if the convention $A > 0$ is used—otherwise $A = -B$ and $\varphi = \pi/2$ is permissible). (2) $a = 0$, $b = -B$. (3) $A = C/\omega$, $\varphi = 0$; $a = C/\omega$, $b = 0$.

E7.28 (1) $A = 0.0201$ m, $\varphi = 5.71$ deg $= 0.0997$ radian.
(2) $x_0 = 0.00173$ m, $v_0 = 0.200$ m/sec.

E7.29 (1) $t' = t + (\varphi/\omega)$. (2) The change of time variable is equivalent to shifting the graph horizontally by $\Delta t = \varphi/\omega$.

E7.31 Sample values:

Height		Mass		Weight
5' 3"	1.60 m	110 lb	49.9 kg	489 N
5' 6"	1.68 m	140 lb	63.5 kg	622 N
5' 9"	1.75 m	170 lb	77.1 kg	756 N
6'	1.83 m	200 lb	90.7 kg	889 N

E7.32 $v_{max} = s_{max}\sqrt{g/\ell} = \theta_{max}\sqrt{g\ell}$. Reasonable values of v_{max}: ~1 to 7 m/sec (for θ_{max} in the range 0.2 to 1 radian and ℓ in the range 2 to 5 m).

E7.33 $v = \omega\sqrt{A^2 - s^2}$.

E7.34 1.00264 sec. <u>Optional</u>: $\Delta T/T = -\frac{1}{2}(\Delta g/g)$.

E7.37 [Uncritical use of Equations 7.71 and 7.74 might cause trouble on this one. In the text, these equations are used at the earth's surface. To generalize them, write $g = g_0(R/r)^2$. Then they become $v = \sqrt{Rg_0(R/r)}$ and $T = 2\pi\sqrt{(R/g_0)(r/R)^3}$ (the latter is Kepler's third law). In going up 100 miles, the changes are $v = -100$ m/sec and $T = 3.2$ min. This is called 4 min near the bottom of p. 235 because of rounding--84.4 and 87.6 min rounded respectively to 84 and 88 min.]

E7.38 (a) $a = \omega v$. (b) $a = 4\pi^2 r/T^2$.

E7.39 5.07×10^3 sec, or 84.4 min.

E7.40 <u>Method 1</u>: Use center-to-center distance for r (not quite correct, but O.K. for this chapter). It gives $a = 2.72 \times 10^{-3}$ m/sec^2 $= 2.78 \times 10^{-4}g = g/3{,}600$.
<u>Method 2</u> (correct): For r, use distance from center of mass to center of moon (3.797×10^8 m, about 2,900 miles less than center-to-center distance). It gives $a = 2.69 \times 10^{-3}$ m/sec^2 $= 2.75 \times 10^{-4}g = g/3{,}640$.

E7.41 $a = 5.93 \times 10^{-3}$ m/sec^2 $= 6.05 \times 10^{-4}g = g/1{,}650$, about 1/6 of the daily-rotation acceleration of the earth's surface.

E7.42 (1) 1.68×10^3 m/sec. (2) 6,480 sec, or 108 min.

E7.43 (1) Zero, since $\mathbf{a} = 0$. (2) 5.4 N, directed toward the center of the circular arc; force supplied by track.

E7.44 (1) 20 m/sec. (2) Speed decreases, angular speed increases.

E7.45 1.96×10^{-15} m. Not significant!

E7.46 1.23 m.

E7.47 22.1 m/sec. 50 m.

E7.48 (1) $v_x = v_{xo} = v_o \cos\theta$, $v_z = v_{zo} - gt = v_o \sin\theta - gt$. (2) $z_{max} = v_{zo}^2/2g = (v_o^2/2g)\sin^2\theta$ ($= \frac{1}{4}\tan\theta \times$ range).

E7.49 (1) $z = (v_{zo}/v_{xo})x - (g/2v_{xo}^2)x^2$.

(2) $z = z_o + (v_{zo}/v_{xo})(x - x_o) - (g/2v_{xo}^2)(x - x_o)^2$

$= [z_o - (v_{zo}x_o/v_{xo}) - (gx_o^2/2v_{xo}^2)] + [(v_{zo}/v_{xo}) + (gx_o/v_{xo}^2)]x - [g/2v_{xo}^2]x^2$.

E7.50 (1) $a_e/a_p = m_p/m_e = 1{,}836$. (2) Opposite directions. $r_e/r_p = \sqrt{m_e/m_p} = 0.0233 = 1/42.8$.

E7.51 (2) $\omega = qB/m$. [The formulas $x = r\cos\omega t$, $y = r\sin\omega t$ given in early printings of the book apply to a negatively charged particle and yield $\omega = -qB/m$. In later printings, the given formulas are $x = r\cos\omega t$, $y = -r\sin\omega t$, leading to $\omega = +qB/m$.]
(4) $r = v/\omega = mv/qB$.

E7.52 (1) $\underset{\sim}{v}' - \underset{\sim}{v} = \underset{\sim}{v}_o$, or $\underset{\sim}{v}' = \underset{\sim}{v} + \underset{\sim}{v}_o$. (2) $\underset{\sim}{a}' = \underset{\sim}{a}$, no difference. (3) Frame S is moving relative to frame S' with constant velocity $\underset{\sim}{v}_o$. At $t = 0$, the origin of frame S is at $\underset{\sim}{r}' = \underset{\sim}{r}_o$.

. . . .

P7.3 (1) T^{-1}. (2) The x coordinate at $t = 0$. (4) mB^2x.

P7.4 (1) $x = x_o + v_o t - (F_o/m\omega^2)\sin\omega t$. [Note that v_o is <u>not</u> $v(0)$]. (2) $x = (F_o/m\omega^2)(\omega t - \sin\omega t)$. The <u>average</u> velocity is constant, which is consistent with zero average force. (More elaborate qualitative explanations are permissible.)
(3) $v(0) = -F_o/m\omega$.

P7.5 (1) (The net force takes the form $F_x = -(k_1 + k_2)x$; then $k = k_1 + k_2$ and $\nu^2 = \nu_1^2 + \nu_2^2$.)
(2) (The net force takes the form $F_x = -(k_1 + k_2) \times (x - x_o)$.)

P7.6 (For $x_o/v_o > 0$, φ lies in the first or third quadrant; for $x_o/v_o < 0$, φ lies in the second or fourth quadrant. The ambiguity is removed with Equation 7.37.)

P7.7 (1) Here is one order-of-magnitude argument, for example: An average speed of the block is $v = \sqrt{2as}$, where a is an average component of acceleration along the trough ($a \ll g$) and s is an average distance moved along the trough. The acceleration in the y direction is approximately a centripetal acceleration: $a_y = v^2/R = 2as/R$ (R is the radius of curvature of the trough). Since $a \ll g$ and $s/R < 1$, then $a_y \ll g$. (2) $k = 2mg\beta$. (3) $T = 2\pi/\sqrt{2g\beta}$.

P7.8 4.91 m.

P7.9 (1) 62.8 m. (2) 2.04 sec. (The time for the ball to catch the stone is $t = \Delta t(v_0 - \frac{1}{2}g\Delta t)/(v_0 - g\Delta t)$, where Δt is the delay time. This becomes infinite for $\Delta t = v_0/g$.)

P7.10 (1)

$$a = \frac{gx_o}{2\ell}(e^{\sqrt{g/\ell}\,t} + e^{-\sqrt{g/\ell}\,t}).$$

[If students need a hint on this one, suggest writing a as a function of x ($a = gx/\ell$) and then either (a) treating this as a differential equation ($d^2x/dt^2 = -gx/\ell$) with exponential solutions or (b) writing $a = v(dv/dx)$ and proceeding in two steps of integration to get v and then x.]
(2) As $x_0 \to 0$, $T \cong \sqrt{\ell/g}\,\ln(2\ell/x_0) \to \infty$ (slowly). As $x_o \to \ell$, $T \cong \sqrt{2(\ell - x_0)/g}$, which is the time of free fall through the small distance $\ell - x_0$.

P7.11 (a) m_0g, constant. (b) $(m_0 + \tau y)g$.
(c) $(m_0 + \tau y)(a + g)$.

P7.12 (1) (Set the change of tension, $\alpha\Delta A$, equal to the change of weight, $\rho gA\Delta y$, or write for the tension, $F_t = Mg + \rho g\int_0^y A(y')\,dy'$. Either approach leads to the differential equation $dA/dy = (\rho g/\alpha)A$.)
(2) (The tension at the bottom of the cable is Mg, so $A_0 = Mg/\alpha$.) (3) $(\alpha/\rho g)\ln 2$.

P7.14 (1) (Write $x = \ell\cos\theta$, $y = \ell\sin\theta$, and differentiate twice with respect to time.)
(2) [An extra for the enterprising student: Explain how these two equations are related to Equations 6.46-6.47 or 6.48-6.49. (Axes 1 and 2 correspond respectively to axes +y' and -x'.)]

P7.15 (1) Since the velocity vector is turning, there is a component of $\underset{\sim}{a}$ perpendicular to $\underset{\sim}{v}$.

P7.16 (1) g at the top, 3g at the bottom.
(2) v(top) = 88.5 m/sec (= 198 mile/hr),
v(bottom) = 153.4 m/sec (= 343 mile/hr).

P7.17 48.5 m/sec, or 108 mile/hr. Yes, he should be concerned.

P7.18 (3) $v = v_0 \sqrt{R/r}$. $\frac{v}{v_0} \cong 1 - \frac{1}{2}\frac{h}{R}$.

P7.19 0.246 mg, horizontal. [Note that the question asks for the net force (which includes gravity). The force supplied by the track is 1.03 mg, at an angle of 13.8 deg to the vertical.]

P7.20 (3) (a) 53.2 deg, or 0.93 radian. (b) 120 sec, or 2 min. (c) 9.55×10^3 m, or 9.55 km, or 5.93 miles. (d) 1.67.

P7.21 (1) $\frac{x^2}{25A^2} + \frac{y^2}{4A^2} = 1.$ An ellipse.

(2) $a_y/a_x = y/x$; the acceleration vector is parallel or antiparallel to the position vector (other facts show it is antiparallel).
(3) $F = m(2\pi/T)^2 \sqrt{x^2 + y^2} = m(2\pi/T)^2 r$; direction is toward the origin ($\underset{\sim}{F} = - m(2\pi/T)^2 \underset{\sim}{r}$).

P7.24 [If the student needs a hint, suggest that he show that the vertical distance between the actual position of the ball (the solid curve) and its projected straight-line path (the dashed line) is the same as the distance the can has fallen at any time.]

P7.26 Optional: (1) (The trajectory equation for $\theta = 45$ deg is $y = x - (g/v_0^2)x^2 = x[1 - (x/R)]$. Set $x = L$ and $y = H$ and solve for R.) He could, of course, hit a ball farther on the moon.
(2) If $L = 415 \pm 2$ ft and $H = 132 \pm 2$ ft, then $R = 609 \pm 9$ ft (estimates of about ± 6 ft to ± 12 ft are acceptable).

P7.27

$$x = x_0 + a \cos \gamma t + b \sin \gamma t,$$
$$y = y_0 - a \sin \gamma t + b \cos \gamma t,$$
$$z = z_0 + v_z t;$$

or

$$x = x_0 + A \sin(\gamma t + \varphi),$$
$$y = y_0 + A \cos(\gamma t + \varphi),$$
$$z = z_0 + v_z t.$$

Note that the x and y equations generalize Equation 6.86 to an offset center of the circle and an arbitrary position on its circumference at t = 0.

P7.28 $D = (eE\ell/mv_o^2)(\frac{1}{2}\ell + L)$. (The terms containing $\frac{1}{2}\ell$ and L correspond respectively to displacements between the plates and beyond the plates.)

P7.29 $\Delta x = \frac{\Delta m}{B}\sqrt{\frac{2dE}{qm}}$.

P7.30 The relative velocity is still the same as in the figure ($\underset{\sim}{v} = v\underset{\sim}{i}$). At t = 0, the origin of frame xy is at $x' = x_o$, $y' = y_o$ and clocks in frame x'y' read $t' = t_o$.

P7.31 (1) $x_C = (v_o - v_C)t + \frac{1}{2}gt^2$ ($= -2t + 4.9t^2$ in SI units). (2) t = 0.408 sec. (3) At $x_A = 2.04$ m. (4) He should throw it upward with an initial speed of 2 m/sec.

P7.32 (1) $z(t) = h + v_o t - \frac{1}{2}gt^2$, $z'(t) = h - \frac{1}{2}gt^2$.
(2) At $z = v_o\sqrt{2h/g}$ at $t = \sqrt{2h/g}$.
(3) At $z' = 0$ at $t = \sqrt{2h/g}$.

P7.33

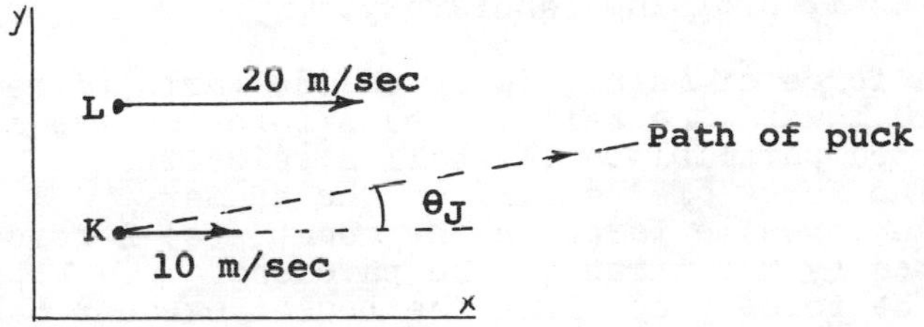

Frame J: $\underset{\sim}{v}_J = 20\underset{\sim}{i} + 2\underset{\sim}{j}$, $v_J = 20.1$ m/sec,
$\theta_J = 5.7$ deg.

Frame K: $\underset{\sim}{v}_K = 10\underset{\sim}{i} + 2\underset{\sim}{j}$, $v_K = 10.2$ m/sec,
$\theta_K = 11.3$ deg.

Frame L: $\underset{\sim}{v}_L = 2\underset{\sim}{j}$, $v_L = 2$ m/sec, $\theta_L = 90$ deg.

CHAPTER 8

Q8.1 (1) Yes or no, depending on student's mass and the assumed mass of the automobile. (Student's top running speed should be 14 to 20 mile/hr. A typical student's momentum can exceed that of a small car (~2,000 lb) but not that of a large car (~4,000 lb).) (2) Very near the speed of light. (A classical calculation with any reasonable parameters gives $v \gg c$.)

Q8.2 Yes for both (assuming prior definitions of mass, velocity, force, and time.)

Q8.4 The speed does not change. Momentum does change.

Q8.5 Doughnut, horseshoe, etc.

Q8.6 (a) At the center. (b) At the center. (c) At the midpoint of its axis. (d) At the center of the hole. (e) On the axis, closer to the bottom than to the top.

Q8.7 At the center of the earth.

Q8.8 The two men separate as their center of mass remains near their orbiting laboratory.

Q8.10 (a) A force of magnitude mg on the earth (directed upward toward the ball). (b) A force on the air directed parallel to the ball's velocity.
(c) The force of the nail on the hammer.
(d) An opposite force on the moon. (e) A force exerted by the tires on the pavement.
(f) The force propelling the rocket exhaust backward.

Q8.12 (1)(a) mg, upward. (b) The same: mg, upward.
(2)(a) Zero. (b) mg, upward (if air friction is ignored).

Q8.13 (2) For Δy arbitrarily small but not zero, the near equality of F_t and F_t' cannot be directly attributed to Newton's third law. Rather, it is attributable to the smallness of the weight of the shaded portion of cable. (Note that two forces governed by Newton's third law are <u>exactly</u> equal in magnitude.) When the limit $\Delta y = 0$ is reached, Newton's third law <u>may</u> be, but need not be, invoked.

Q8.14 (The spontaneous acceleration of isolated bodies is one important point.)

Q8.15 In both cases, the center of mass follows a parabolic trajectory as if all the mass were concentrated there.

Q8.16 Any system that includes the student and excludes the earth. Any system that includes both the student and the earth.

Q8.17 The center-of-mass velocity remains constant.

Q8.18 (If the third law failed for interatomic forces, the first law would fail for bodies composed of atoms. A system obeys the first law because its parts obey the third law.)

Q8.20 No. A motionless third particle could have been created.

Q8.21 No. One or more neutral particles (leaving no tracks) might have been created.

Q8.23 (1) It says only that their total momentum remains zero (or their center of mass remains at rest). (2) No (although the momentum of the two balls might change if they interact with something else during their collision).

Q8.24 The change of momentum of the whole system during the collision is small in comparison with the change of momentum of one of the colliding objects.

Q8.25 Let $\mathbf{r}$ and $\mathbf{p}$ define a plane. Since the component of the force $\mathbf{F}$ perpendicular to the plane is zero, the component of $\mathbf{p}$ perpendicular to the plane is constant: it is initially zero and remains zero.

Q8.26 (1) For another reason: The external forces acting on him sum to zero. (2) No. [A suggested helpful comparison: Consider a falling body that fragments into many smaller bodies, all of which fall more slowly. The total momentum of the system evidently decreases.]

Q8.27 (2) No.

Q8.29 The change Δv does <u>not</u> depend on v_0. The fractional change <u>does</u> depend on v_0.

Q8.30 [At least two have been discussed: radiation pressure (solar sailing) and gravitational acceleration by the moon or other planets (see Problem 12.30).]

. . . .

E8.1 (a) $p = mv_0 + mgt = p_0 + mgt$.

(b) $p = m\sqrt{v_0^2 + 2gs} = \sqrt{p_0^2 + 2m^2gs}$.

E8.2 (1) 1.7×10^{-20} kg m/sec. (2) 5×10^{-15} kg m/sec^2. (3) 3.4×10^{-6} sec (3.4 μsec).

E8.3 (a) 4.5×10^{-24} kg m/sec, horizontally to the right. (b) 1.5×10^{-24} kg m/sec, horizontally to the right. (c) 3.35×10^{-24} kg m/sec, upward to the right at an angle of 26.6 deg to the horizontal.

E8.5 (1) 120 N. (2) 6.25 sec.

E8.6 (1) $m\mathbf{v}$ to the struck marble, $-m\mathbf{v}$ to the incident marble. (2) Zero.

E8.7 (1)(a) 8,485 kg m/sec (or N sec), directed southeastward. (b) 6,000 kg m/sec (or N sec), directed westward. (2) 1,700 N, directed southeastward.

E8.8 (1) $d\mathbf{p}/dt = m(d\mathbf{v}/dt) + (dm/dt)\mathbf{v}$. (2) (An airplane, for example, as its fuel is consumed.)

E8.10 (a) $\overline{x} = x_0 + \frac{1}{2}v_0(t_2 + t_1) + (a/6)(t_2^2 + t_2t_1 + t_1^2)$,

$\overline{v} = v_0 + \frac{1}{2}a(t_2 + t_1)$. (b) $\overline{x} = (a/6)T^2$, $\overline{v} = \frac{1}{2}aT$.

E8.11 (1) At $x = 5$, $y = 2$. (2) At $x = 3$, $y = 2$.

E8.12 (1) On a line between the centers, 0.646 Å from the center of the C atom and 0.484 Å from the center of the O atom. (2) Upward at a speed of 225 m/sec.

E8.14 $v_c = [m_1/(m_1 + m_2)]v_1$, $a_c = 0$.

E8.15 (a) $\mathbf{r}_c = (v_0t/3)(2\mathbf{i} - \mathbf{j})$. (b) $\mathbf{v}_c = (v_0/3)(2\mathbf{i} - \mathbf{j})$. (c) $\mathbf{a}_c = 0$.

E8.16 $\mathbf{v}_c = v_0\mathbf{i} + \frac{1}{2}(v_1 - gt)\mathbf{j}$, $\mathbf{a}_c = -\frac{1}{2}g\mathbf{j}$.

E8.17 (1)(a) $\mathbf{P} = 2mv_0\mathbf{i} + m(v_1 - gt)\mathbf{j}$. (b) $d\mathbf{P}/dt = -mg\mathbf{j}$. (2) $-mg\mathbf{j}$.

E8.18 (1) The center of mass is accelerated in the direction of the thrust. (2) $|\Delta\mathbf{v}| = 0.4$ m/sec.

E8.19 (1) Let $M = m_1 + m_2$. (a) $v_c = g[t - (m_2/M)t_1]$.

(b) $a_c = g$. (c) $P = Mgt - m_2gt_1$. (d) $F = Mg$.

E8.20 9.8×10^4 N.

E8.21 (a) 98 N (mg), upward. (b) 98 N (mg), upward. (c) 1.96×10^4 N (200mg), downward. (d) Zero.

E8.22 2.68×10^{-22} m/sec^2. 1.73×10^{-15} m, less than the diameter of a nucleus (about the diameter of a single proton).

E8.24 Upward force of upper link, 236 N; downward force of lower link, 118 N; downward force of gravity, 98 N; total force (upward), 20 N.

E8.25 (1) $(N - n)(ma + F_f)$. (2) $(N - n)(ma + F_f)$. (3) $N(ma + F_f)$.

E8.26 (1) 20 N, forward. (2) 1.25 m/sec^2. (3)(a) 20 N. (b) 20 N.

E8.27 2.47×10^5 m/sec, at 45 deg to the initial direction of the alpha particle.

E8.28 (1) 5.89×10^{-20} kg m/sec, directed at 30 deg to the initial pion direction and 120 deg to the other photon direction. (2) 2.13×10^8 m/sec (0.71c). Optional: 1.73×10^8 m/sec (0.578c).

E8.29 Zero.

E8.30 (2) It is valid when the two objects are free of outside forces. (3) The vertical components of force on the carts sum to zero. The horizontal components of force are negligible.

E8.31 1.067 m/sec.

E8.32 47.3 mile/hr, in the direction in which the truck was moving. $|\Delta \underset{\sim}{v}(\text{truck})| = 12.7$ mile/hr, $|\Delta \underset{\sim}{v}(\text{car})| = 127$ mile/hr.

E8.33 0.129 m/sec.

E8.34 (1) 2.33 kg m/sec, 13.3 percent of original momentum. (2) Momentum was imparted to the air.

E8.35 (a) 6.025 m/sec. (b) 6.00 m/sec (if frictional forces prevent skidding to the side).

E8.36 188 m/sec.

E8.37 12.5 mile/hr (5.59 m/sec), directed 36.9 deg north of east (53.1 deg east of north). It is the same before, during, and after the collision.

E8.38 (1) $v_2 = 3.46 \times 10^6$ m/sec, $v_3 = 2 \times 10^6$ m/sec.
(2) Yes.

E8.39 (2) In the "stationary" frame of reference, the speed of the exhaust gas varies during the interval considered. Only for $\Delta v \ll v_{ex}$ can this variation be ignored.

E8.40 0.2 percent.

E8.41 $m_2 = m_1 e^{-(v_2 - v_1)/v_{ex}}$. (a) For $\Delta v \ll v_{ex}$, $m_2 \cong m_1[1 - (\Delta v/v_{ex})$; a small fractional change of mass. (b) For $\Delta v \gg v_{ex}$, $m_2 = m_1 e^{-\Delta v/v_{ex}} \cong 0$; almost all mass must be ejected.

E8.42 (1) 588 kg/sec. (2) 6.47×10^4 kg. 12.9 m/sec^2, or 1.32g.

E8.44 (2) (Write $\mu = m(M - m)/M$, with M fixed and m variable; differentiate and set $d\mu/dm = 0$.)
(3) (Start with the exact expression $\mu = m_1/[1 + (m_1/m_2)]$.)

. . . .

P8.1 (1) $d\underset{\sim}{p}/dt = \underset{\sim}{F} = F_o\underset{\sim}{j}$. (2) F_o/p_o (radian/sec).
(3) Zero. (4) The first ($d\underset{\sim}{p}/dt$) will remain constant; the other two will change.

P8.2 (1) 6.525 kg m/sec (approximately horizontal).
(2) 4.97 kg m/sec (at 45 deg to the horizontal).
(3)(a) $\underset{\sim}{I} = 10.04\underset{\sim}{i} + 3.52\underset{\sim}{j}$ ($\underset{\sim}{i}$ is horizontal, directed from home plate to center field; $\underset{\sim}{j}$ is vertically upward; the unit is kg m/sec, or N sec). Magnitude, 10.64 kg m/sec; angle, 19.3 deg to the horizontal.
(b) The negative of the above vector.
(4) $\overline{F} = I/\Delta t$, about 10^4 N for $\Delta t = 10^{-3}$ sec, for example. [The student may find it hard to believe that Δt is 10^{-3} sec or less. Suggest that he or she guess the distance that the center of mass of the ball moves as it is being slowed from 45 m/sec to rest, calculate the time required for this deceleration, and double this time to get Δt.]

P8.4 (a) $\underset{\sim}{r}_c = (5/6)\underset{\sim}{i} + \underset{\sim}{j}$ (m). (b) $\underset{\sim}{v}_c$ = constant; its magnitude and direction cannot be determined.
(c) $\underset{\sim}{a}_c = 0$. (d) Nothing can be said about the velocities of the three objects. (e) $\underset{\sim}{a}_3 = -5\underset{\sim}{i} - 3\underset{\sim}{j}$ (m/sec^2).

P8.5 (1)(a) 216 N. (b) 216 N. (c) 240 N. (d) 19.6 N.
(2)(a) 98 N. (b) 98 N. (c) 110 N.

P8.6 (1) αv. (2) αvt, the impulse delivered by the belt to the sawdust and also the total momentum of the sawdust on the belt.

P8.7 (1) $F(t) = nmv_0 + nmg(t - t_1) + Mg$.
(2)

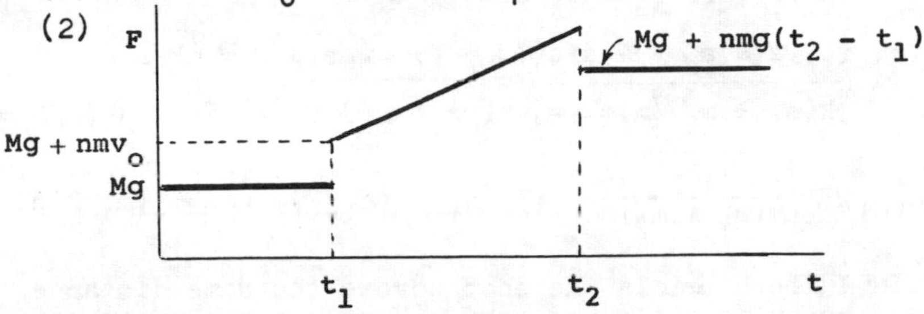

P8.9 (1) $m_1 = 2.98$ (approximately 3) kg, $m_2 = 5.02$ (approximately 5) kg. (2) 4.5 revolutions.
[<u>Note</u>: In early printings of the text, the v_2 arrow is incorrectly shown pointing upward. It should point downward.]

P8.10 (1) (The tension in each string is $mg/\cos\theta$. Its vertical component cancels the force of gravity on a ball. Its horizontal component is $mg \tan\theta$.) (2) Horizontal. (3) $\ell(1 - \cos\theta_0)$.

P8.11 (1) $v = [m/(M_1 + M_2 + m)]v_0$. (2) 0.599 m/sec.
(3) $v'(\text{between}) = v_0 - (M_1/m)v =$
$[(M_2 + m)/(M_1 + M_2 + m)]v_0 = 300.3$ m/sec.

P8.12 (1) 39.92 m/sec. (2)(a) 0.0798 m/sec.
(b) 0.1592 m/sec. (The speed of the batted ball relative to the ice is 39.84 m/sec. The recoil speed of the batter is 0.1595 m/sec.)

P8.13 (1) $v = v_0 \cos\theta$.

P8.14 $\dfrac{dv}{dm} = -\dfrac{v_{ex}}{m} - g\dfrac{dt}{dm}$, or $\dfrac{dv}{dt} = -\dfrac{v_{ex}}{m}\dfrac{dm}{dt} - g$.

$v_2 - v_1 = v_{ex}\ln(m_1/m_2) - g(t_2 - t_1)$.

P8.15 (2) (For thrust equal to weight, $m = m_0 e^{-t/\mathcal{J}}$.)

P8.16 (1) Equations 8.79 and 8.80 require no change. The other four are changed as follows:

$$\mathbf{r}_1 = \mathbf{r}_c - (m_2/M)\mathbf{r}, \qquad \mathbf{r}_2 = \mathbf{r}_c + (m_1/M)\mathbf{r},$$
$$\mathbf{v}_1 = \mathbf{v}_c - (m_2/M)\mathbf{v}, \qquad \mathbf{v}_2 = \mathbf{v}_c + (m_1/M)\mathbf{r}.$$

(2) The one-particle momentum, $\mathbf{p} = \mu\mathbf{v}$, can be written $\mathbf{p} = \mathbf{p}_2 - (m_2/M)\mathbf{P}$, where $\mathbf{P}$ is the constant total momentum of the system. Therefore $d\mathbf{p}/dt = d\mathbf{p}_2/dt$, so $\mathbf{F}_2 = d\mathbf{p}/dt$.

P8.17 (1) $s = s_o + A\sin(\omega t + \varphi)$, where $\omega = \sqrt{k/\mu} = \sqrt{k(m_1 + m_2)/m_1 m_2} = \sqrt{k(\frac{1}{m_1} + \frac{1}{m_2})}$. (2) $T = 2\pi\sqrt{\mu/k} = 2\pi\sqrt{\dfrac{m_1 m_2}{k(m_1 + m_2)}}$. (3) $s_1 = (m_2/M)s$, $s_2 = (m_1/M)s$.

P8.18 In both trials the shot covers the same distance measured along the car. (Here are two among several possible explanations: 1. For both trials, the flatcar defines an inertial frame of reference. In these respective frames, the laws of motion are the same and the initial conditions are the same, so the trajectory and the range are the same. 2. Use an earth-based frame for both trials. The vertical component of motion is not influenced by the recoil, so the time of flight is the same for both trials. In this time the shot moves through a horizontal distance $v_x t$ when the car is locked. When the car recoils, the shot moves forward a lesser distance $(v_x - v_R)t$ while the car is moving backward a distance $v_R t$. Relative to the car, the shot covers the same distance $v_x t$.)

P8.19 (1) $m_1 v_o = m_1 v_1 + m_2 v_2$. (3)

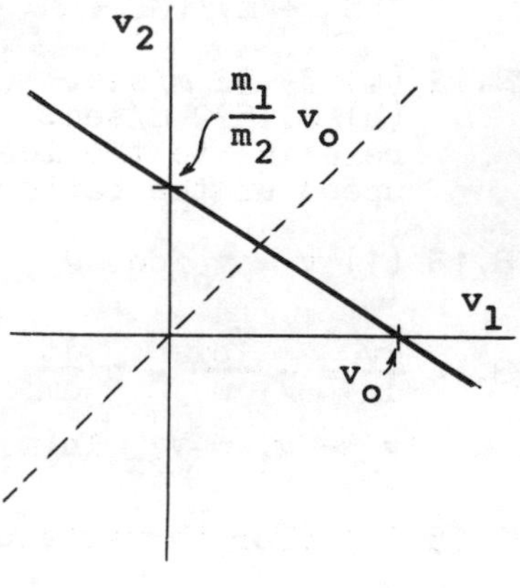

(2) It is valid for both.
(4) Impenetrability means $v_2 \geqslant v_1$; this defines the region above and to the left of the dashed line.
(5) $v_1(\max) = [m_1/(m_1 + m_2)]v_o$,
$v_1(\min) = -\infty$.
$v_2(\max) = +\infty$,
$v_2(\min) = [m_1/(m_1 + m_2)]v_o$.

P8.20 (1) The total momenta in the two frames differ by the constant $M\underset{\sim}{v}_0$ (where $M = \sum_i m_i$), so $d\underset{\sim}{P}/dt = d\underset{\sim}{P}'/dt$.
(2) The quantity is not invariant; the law is invariant.

CHAPTER 9

Q9.2 Angular momentum of the main rotor is upward. Angular momentum of the tail rotor is horizontal, directed to the right side of the craft. The total angular momentum is directed generally upward, inclined slightly to the right side.

Q9.3 (a) Yes. (b) No.

Q9.4 (a) If its velocity is zero. (b) Under no conditions for a classical point particle. (However, a spinning particle or spinning body has nonzero angular momentum with respect to all reference points.)

Q9.5 (1)(a) Any point on its path. (b) Any point not on its path. (2) No.

Q9.6 Defined with respect to an origin: (a), (e). Independent of the choice of origin: (b), (c), (d), (f).

Q9.7 (1) No. (2) Yes.

Q9.8 (1)(a) Vertically upward. (b) Horizontal, directed from the car to the center of the track.
(2) The outer wheels (those on the right side of the car).

Q9.9 (1) Spin. (2) A combination of both.

Q9.13 Infinitely many: all lines in the plane of the hoop that pass through its center and one axial line perpendicular to the plane of the hoop.

Q9.14 Infinitely many: the axis of cylindrical symmetry (perpendicular to the flat ends of the can) and all lines passing through the center of the can in a plane perpendicular to the cylindrical axis.

Q9.15 (1) External torques are negligible.
(2) The angular velocity is not parallel to a symmetry axis. (3) The passer has given the ball an angular velocity that is parallel to its axis of cylindrical symmetry.

Q9.16 (2) kg m^2/sec^2. Torque and energy have the same dimension.

Q9.20 For each contributing force, $\underset{\sim}{F}_i$ is parallel to $\underset{\sim}{r}_i$, so $\underset{\sim}{T}_i = 0$.

Q9.23 (1) They precess at the same rate.
(2) The wheel with the more uniform mass distribution precesses more rapidly.

Q9.25 (1) The increasing angular momentum of the engine is partially compensated by an opposite angular momentum of the car. (2) No, not conserved. An external torque acts (from unequal vertical forces on the tires). (3) Yes, with two counter-rotating crankshafts (or possibly a vertical crankshaft).

Q9.26 He does not stop turning, but his angular speed decreases markedly.

Q9.27 [Suggestion: Let a student on a turntable, starting from rest with zero angular momentum, practice turning to a new direction and stopping there.]

Q9.29 Yes, in principle, the day becomes slightly longer. The moment of inertia of the earth increases and its angular speed decreases.

Q9.30 As he pedals, he and the bicycle do backward somersaults. Angular momentum is conserved. When he brakes and the wheels stop, he also stops, not necessarily at his original orientation.

Q9.31 (1) He does not turn. (2) He turns in the original direction of the wheel's rotation (counterclockwise as seen from above). (3) He stops turning.
(4) He turns in the same direction as in part 2, but only half as fast.

Q9.32 Yes, by changing its moment of inertia. ("No" is an acceptable answer if the body is assumed to be a rigid body.)

Q9.33 $2\hbar$.

Q9.34 She exerts a vertical torque (downward), so the angular momentum vector starts to rotate from a horizontal direction toward a vertical direction.
(2) No. (3) The left handle "wants" to go up, the right handle "wants" to go down.

Q9.35 Yes. (Moving in a central field of force, a particle has constant angular momentum with respect to the force center and variable angular momentum with respect to other points.)

Q9.37 (2) Yes. Effects associated with centrifugal and coriolis forces. [The student can describe one or more such effects without knowing these names.]

Q9.38 Radical: Angular momentum is not conserved and/or internal torques do not sum to zero. Conservative: The room is experiencing angular acceleration.

. . . .

E9.1 (2) $L = |L_z|$. L and L_z may differ in sign.

E9.2 (a) 1.67×10^{-18} kg m^2/sec, directed upward from the page. (b) 8.35×10^{-18} kg m^2/sec, directed upward from the page. (c) Zero.

E9.3 (2) A polar vector.

E9.4 (a) Electrons or other elementary particles; also atoms and molecules. (b) Spinning macroscopic objects such as baseballs, bowling balls, etc. (c) The earth (with respect to its own center).

E9.5 (2)(a) p, $r_\perp$. (b) r, p, $r_\perp$, $v_\perp$. (c) r, $r_\perp$.

E9.6 $L = 2\pi mR^2 \cos^2\theta/T$.

E9.7 (2)(a) P farther than Q from the path.
(b) P closer than Q to the path.
(c) P and Q equidistant from the path.
(d) P and Q both on the path.

E9.8 (1) Downward into the page. (2) mv_0b.
(3) $v/v_0 = 0.5$.

E9.10 (1) It is a sine function in the xy plane ($y = A \sin kx$, where $k = \omega/v_0$).
(2) $L_z = mAv_0(\omega t \cos \omega t - \sin \omega t)$.
(3) At $t = n\pi/\omega$ (n is a positive or negative integer or zero), at $x = n\pi v_0/\omega$, $y = 0$ (the equally spaced points where the particle crosses the x axis).

E9.11 This result states that $\underset{\sim}{r}_c' = 0$, where $\underset{\sim}{r}_c'$ is the position vector of the center of mass relative to the center of mass (necessarily zero!).

E9.12 (1) $\underset{\sim}{r}_c = a\underset{\sim}{i}$. (2) $\underset{\sim}{v}_c = 0$. (3) $L_{1z} = -mv_0b$, $L_{2z} = mv_0a$, $L_{3z} = mv_0(2a + b)$, $L_{4z} = mv_0a$; $L_{Tz} = 4mv_0a$. (4) The total angular momentum is independent of b because the center of mass is at rest (the system as a whole has only spin angular momentum, which is independent of the choice of reference point).

E9.13 (1) 2v. (2) 2mvd. (3) In A's frame of reference, the center of mass of the system is <u>not</u> at rest, so the theorem in Section 9.2 does not apply.

E9.14 (1) $\underset{\sim}{r}_c = \frac{1}{2}d\underset{\sim}{j}$, $\underset{\sim}{v}_c = v_0\underset{\sim}{j}$. (2) $\underset{\sim}{L}_{orbital} = 0$, $\underset{\sim}{L}_{spin} = \underset{\sim}{L}_{total} = -\, mdv_0\underset{\sim}{k}$.

E9.15 $\underset{\sim}{L}_{orbital} = -\, Mv_0y_0\underset{\sim}{k} = -\, 20\underset{\sim}{k}$ kg m^2/sec, $\underset{\sim}{L}_{spin} = -\, 20\underset{\sim}{k}$ kg m^2/sec, $\underset{\sim}{L}_{total} = -\, 40\underset{\sim}{k}$ kg m^2/sec.

E9.16 The moon. [$L_M'/L_E' = m_E/m_M = 81.4$; primes denote values relative to the center of mass. See also Problem 9.5.]

E9.17 (1)(a) $L_{orbital} = ma^2\omega$. (b) $L_{spin} = 0$.
(2) $L_{orbital} = 0$, $L_{spin} = 2ma^2\omega$. (In the first case, the center of mass of the "system" is moving. In the second case, it is not moving.)

E9.18 (1) $6\hbar$ (6.33×10^{-34} kg m^2/sec). (2) $7\hbar$.

E9.19 (1) $\omega = v/r = 3$ radian/sec. (2) 0.15 kg m^2/sec.

E9.20 (2) $\omega = v_c/r$, $\alpha = a_c/r$.

E9.21 (1) 5.65 kg m^2/sec, vertical. (2) 0.942 kg m^2/sec, horizontal.

E9.22 Yes.

E9.23 Set a = R and write $dm = \tau\, ds$, where $\tau = M/2\pi R$ = mass per unit length around the hoop. Then

$$I = R^2\tau\int_0^{2\pi R} ds = 2\pi R^3\tau = MR^2.$$

E9.24 $I = MR^2$.

E9.25 $I = 2ma^2$ (independent of ℓ).

E9.27 (1) 30 deg. (2) They extend the same distance from the axis.

E9.28 (1) 0.224 m. (2) 0.158 m. (3) It must have more mass per unit area near its center than near its edge.

E9.29 (1)(a) 0.0960 m. (b) 0.0368 kg m^2.
(2) 0.343 m. 0.589 kg m^2.

E9.31 $I = \frac{1}{12}Ma^2$.

E9.32 $I = \frac{1}{2}M(a^2 + b^2)$.

E9.33 (1) $L = \frac{1}{2}m\ell^2\omega$, $I = \frac{1}{2}m\ell^2$. (2) $L_{spin} = L_{orbital} = \frac{1}{2}m\ell^2\omega$, $L_{total} = m\ell^2\omega$, $I = m\ell^2$. [See the parallel-axis theorem in Problem 9.14.]

E9.34 (1) $L_{orbital} = MR^2\omega$, $L_{total} = (7/5)MR^2\omega$.
(2) $I = (7/5)MR^2$. A factor of 3.5.

E9.35 An angle of 41.8 deg to the radial line (or 48.2 deg to the tangent line).

E9.36 (1) 125 N m. (2) 8,333 N. (3) By moving his hands farther from the axis, yes. By changing the directions, no.

E9.37 (1) Zero. (2) 15.8 kg m^2/sec. (3) Gravity exerts a torque on the ball with respect to a reference point at the boy. [See also Problem 9.17.]

E9.38 (1) 1.35 kg m^2/sec. (2) 0.75 radian/sec.

E9.39 (1)(a) $k = r$. (b) $k = r/\sqrt{2} = 0.707r$.
(c) $k = \sqrt{0.4}\,r = 0.632r$. (2) It is the radius of a hoop that has the same mass and the same moment of inertia as the object being considered.

E9.40 $\omega^2 - \omega_0^2 = 2\alpha(\theta - \theta_0)$.

E9.41 (a) 75 radian/sec. (b) 3 radian/sec^2.
(c) 149.2 revolutions. (d) 1.35×10^4 kg m^2/sec.
(e) 540 N m. (f) 2,700 N.

E9.42 (1) 4.9 N m. (2) 0.408 radian, or 23.4 deg.
(3) Yes ($L_{orbital}$ = 0.0408 kg m^2/sec).

E9.43 (1) 400 kg m^2/sec. (2) Yes.

E9.44 (1) $\omega_f = \omega/17 = 0.0588\omega$. (2) No. The frictional forces are internal forces and produce no net torque. [But kinetic energy is not conserved.]

E9.45 (1) 0.96 kg m^2/sec. (2) (Example: m = 70 kg, k (the radius of gyration--see Exercise 9.39) = 0.2 m, $I = mk^2$ = 2.8 kg m^2, $\omega = L/I$ = 0.34 radian/sec. Answers in the range 0.1 to 1 radian/sec are reasonable.)

E9.46 (1) Very roughly, a doubling of ω (answers in the range 7 to 15 radian/sec are reasonable).

(2) Yes, because of the importance of the r^2 factor in the formula $I = mr^2$. (Example: $m = 4$ kg, $r = 0.8$ m, $I = 2.56$ kg m^2. The moment of inertia of the weights alone is comparable to that of the student if he is standing over the axis with his arms in.)

E9.47 $v = 19v_0$. [$v = (a + c)/(a - c) = (1 + e)/(1 - e)$.]

E9.48 1.027.

E9.49 (At apogee, $dr/dt = 0$. If $\underset{\sim}{v}$ is not perpendicular to $\underset{\sim}{r}$, the component v_r is not zero, which means $dr/dt \neq 0$.)

. . . .

P9.1 (1) (It is an ellipse centered at the origin.) (2) $\underset{\sim}{r} = a \cos \omega t\, \underset{\sim}{i} + b \sin \omega t\, \underset{\sim}{j}$, $\underset{\sim}{v} = - a\omega \sin \omega t\, \underset{\sim}{i} + b\omega \cos \omega t\, \underset{\sim}{j}$. (4) $A = \pi ab$.

P9.2 (1) $\underset{\sim}{L} = m\omega b(a + d \cos \omega t)\underset{\sim}{k}$.

(2) $\underset{\sim}{T} = - m\omega^2 bd \sin \omega t\, \underset{\sim}{k}$. (3) Maximum L (= $2mab\omega$) at $\underset{\sim}{r} = a\underset{\sim}{i}$; minimum L (= 0) at $\underset{\sim}{r} = - a\underset{\sim}{i}$. Maximum T (= $mab\omega^2$) at $r = \pm b\underset{\sim}{j}$; minimum T (= 0) at $\underset{\sim}{r} = \pm a\underset{\sim}{i}$. [Note: The student might seek maxima and minima of L_z and T_z instead of L and T. The answers for L_z and L are the same. The answers for T_z are maximum T_z (= $mab\omega^2$) at $\underset{\sim}{r} = - b\underset{\sim}{j}$; minimum T_z (= $- mab\omega^2$) at $\underset{\sim}{r} = b\underset{\sim}{j}$. All answers assume positive a and b.]

P9.3 (2) $\underset{\sim}{L} = mad\omega(5 \sin \omega t \cos 5\omega t - \cos \omega t \sin 5\omega t)\underset{\sim}{i}$
$- mad\omega(\sin \omega t \sin 5\omega t + 5 \cos \omega t \cos 5\omega t)\underset{\sim}{j}$
$+ ma^2\omega\underset{\sim}{k}$.

(3) ($L^2 = m^2a^2\omega^2[a^2 + d^2(1 + 24 \cos^2 5\omega t)]$.)

P9.4 (2) It is at rest.

P9.5 (1) $\underset{\sim}{L}_1 = m_1r_1v_1\underset{\sim}{k} = (m_1m_2{}^2/M^2)r^2\omega\underset{\sim}{k}$ (where $M = m_1 + m_2$), $\underset{\sim}{L}_2 = m_2r_2v_2\underset{\sim}{k} = (m_2m_1{}^2/M^2)r^2\omega\underset{\sim}{k}$; $L_1/L_2 = m_2/m_1$. (<u>Optional</u>: Write $\underset{\sim}{L} = m_1\underset{\sim}{r}_1 \times \underset{\sim}{v}_1 + m_2\underset{\sim}{r}_2 \times \underset{\sim}{v}_2$ and use Equations 8.75–8.78 to substitute for $\underset{\sim}{r}_1$, $\underset{\sim}{v}_1$, $\underset{\sim}{r}_2$, and $\underset{\sim}{v}_2$.)

P9.6 $L_{orbital} = 2mr^2 \cos^2\frac{1}{2}\theta\, \omega$, $L_{spin} = 2mr^2 \sin^2\frac{1}{2}\theta\, \omega$, $L_{total} = 2mr^2\omega$. For $\theta = 0$, $L_{spin} = 0$; for $\theta = \pi$,

$L_{orbital} = 0$. (The distance from the origin to the center of mass is $r \cos \frac{1}{2}\theta$. The line joining the two weights has length $2r \sin \frac{1}{2}\theta$ and rotates at angular speed ω.)

P9.7 (2) Yes. Yes.

P9.8 $I = \frac{1}{12}M\ell^2 + Mx^2$.

P9.10 (a) $(1/6)M\ell^2$. (b) $(5/12)M\ell^2$. (c) $(1/6)M\ell^2$.

P9.13 ($\underset{\sim}{r}_c \times \underset{\sim}{v}_c$ is parallel to $\underset{\sim}{\omega}$, so $\underset{\sim}{L}_{orbital}$ is parallel to $\underset{\sim}{\omega}$. $\underset{\sim}{L}_{spin}$ is also parallel to $\underset{\sim}{\omega}$.)

P9.17 (1) $x(t) = v_0 t \cos \theta$, $y(t) = v_0 t \sin \theta - \frac{1}{2}gt^2$, $v_x(t) = v_0 \cos \theta$, $v_y(t) = v_0 \sin \theta - gt$.
(2) $\underset{\sim}{L} = -\frac{1}{2}mv_0 gt^2 \cos \theta \, \underset{\sim}{k}$. (3) $\underset{\sim}{T} = -mv_0 gt \cos \theta \, \underset{\sim}{k}$.
(4) The same as in part 2.

P9.18 (1) ($\underset{\sim}{T} = d\underset{\sim}{L}/dt$ is true in general, but $\underset{\sim}{L} = I\underset{\sim}{\omega}$ and $d\underset{\sim}{L}/dt = I\underset{\sim}{\alpha}$ are true only for principal axes.)
(2) $T_z = I\alpha$.

P9.19 It moves opposite to the direction of the applied impulse. [Method 1: The impulse gives the pole a momentum p ($p = mv_c$) and an angular momentum L relative to its center of mass ($L = \frac{1}{2}\ell p$, where ℓ is the length of the pole). The angular speed of the pole can then be calculated to be $\omega = 6v_c/\ell$, so that the ends of the pole move at speed $3v_c$ relative to the center. Relative to the ground, the upper end moves forward at speed $4v_c$ and the lower end moves backward at speed $2v_c$. Method 2: Imagine the rod to be pivoted at its lower end. A force parallel to the applied force must act at the pivot to make the pole's rotation and the motion of its center of mass consistent. Without such a force, the bottom of the pole moves backward. Method 3: Seek a pivot point at which no additional force need be applied. This point is at distance $\ell/3$ above the ground. It is the point that is motionless just after the blow.

P9.20 (1) $a_c = (F_1 + F_2)/M$. $\alpha = (F_1 - F_2)r/I$.

(3) $\dfrac{F_2}{F_1} = \dfrac{(r/k)^2 - 1}{(r/k)^2 + 1}$.

P9.21 $\frac{F_2}{F_1} = - \frac{1}{1 + (Mr^2/I)}$.

P9.22 $a_c = g \sin \theta/[1 + (I/Mr^2)]$; the acceleration of a body sliding without friction is $g \sin \theta$. (For a hoop, $a_c = \frac{1}{2}g \sin \theta$. For a uniform cylinder, $a_c = (2/3)g \sin \theta$.)

P9.23 (2) (Note that $d\mathbf{L}_{orbital}/dt = 0$ because $\mathbf{L}_{orbital}$ is constant, and $\boldsymbol{\omega}_p \times \mathbf{L}_{orbital} = 0$ because $\boldsymbol{\omega}_p$ and $\mathbf{L}_{orbital}$ are parallel.)

P9.24 (2) T is proportional to $\sin \alpha$; ω_p is independent of α.

P9.26 (1) $4\omega_0$. (2) The constancy of L means $\omega \sim 1/r^2$. The centripetal acceleration is $a = \omega^2 r \sim 1/r^3$. The contraction cannot continue indefinitely; the required centripetal force increases faster than the available gravitational force.

P9.27 (1) Forces of gravity and the force supporting the pulley. They <u>can</u> sum to zero but <u>need</u> <u>not</u> sum to zero. (2) Zero. (3) The speed of the rope is v; it moves up on the left, down on the right. (The speed of the counterweight is v; the speed of the monkey relative to the rope is 2v.)

P9.28 (1)(a) 2mg. (b) 2mg. (c) Zero (neglecting the weight of the pulley). (2) They reach the floor together.

P9.29 (1) $mgr\mathbf{k}$ (r is the radius of the pulley and $\mathbf{k}$ is a unit vector directed into the page).
(2) $\mathbf{L} = mgrt\mathbf{k}$. (3) Yes. He must accelerate downward with $a \cong \frac{1}{2}g$. (4) If the monkey moves upward, the counterweight will move upward faster and it will reach the pulley first. If the counterweight sticks at the pulley, the problem is changed, and the monkey can then climb to the pulley. If the counterweight goes over the pulley, the monkey can never reach the pulley.

P9.30 (1) Relative to the force center, the total torque on the planet is zero; therefore $\mathbf{L}$ = constant. The torque is also zero relative to the center of mass of the planet; therefore $\mathbf{L}_{spin}$ = constant.
(2) Relative to the center of mass of the planet, the torque need not be zero, so $\mathbf{L}_{spin}$ need not be constant. The total angular momentum (relative to

the force center) is still constant. [See also Figure 11.9 and the discussion on p. 456 of the text.]

CHAPTER 10

Q10.2 (1) The net displacement is zero (refer to Equation 10.1). (2) Equation 10.1 is still applicable. (3) Negative.

Q10.4 (1) Yes, in a special case (assuming prior definitions of force and displacement). (2) By definition. (3) True scalar.

Q10.5 (a) $K = p^2/2m$. (b) $K = \frac{1}{2}pv$.

Q10.7 (a) m and K. (Measured value of v_x would differ in general but could be the same in special cases—if $\mathbf{v} = 0$ or if the x and x' axes were parallel). (b) m. (Measured values of K and/or v_x could be the same in special cases.)

Q10.8 (1) $\mathbf{F}$ and $d\mathbf{s}$ are perpendicular at all times; $\mathbf{F} \cdot d\mathbf{s} = 0$. (2) Constant: m, K, $\mathbf{T}$, $\mathbf{L}$; magnitudes of $\mathbf{r}$, $\mathbf{v}$, p, $\mathbf{F}$, $\mathbf{a}$ (the star is at the origin). Variable: $\mathbf{r}$, $\mathbf{v}$, $\mathbf{p}$, $\mathbf{F}$, $\mathbf{a}$.

Q10.9 (1) - 10 MeV. (2) Zero.

Q10.10 Rocket thrust, yes (positive). Air friction, yes (negative). All forces combined, no.

Q10.11 Two particles with $\mathbf{v}_1 = -\mathbf{v}_2$ moving along the same straight line.

Q10.12 The net work is zero.

Q10.13 No. The positive work done by the man's hands is compensated by a negative work done by internal forces in the spring. (The spring experiences no change of total kinetic energy.) [If the potential-energy concept replaces the concept of internal work, so that only external work is considered, the answer would be yes.]

Q10.14 (1) Not necessarily (it may be zero in a special case). (2) Only from before to after.

Q10.15 Yes. [Note that this is physically equivalent to a child on a swing; air friction plays no important role in enabling the child to swing.]

Q10.16 (a) Kinetic energy of the ball. (b) Heating of the mitt (increased internal energy). (c) Increased internal energy of air and pump. (d) Increased potential energy. (e) Increased kinetic energy.

Q10.18 (1) More force. (2) Yes, but some of the output work appears as kinetic energy of the load. [See also Problem 10.5.]

Q10.20 Examples: torque (through a gear train), speed (pivoted bar, or fluid in a pipe), angular speed.

Q10.21 $F_1 < F_2 < F_3$. None are equal.

Q10.23 (1) Gravity. (2) Frictional forces of air and road and the normal contact force at the road. (3) Constant: (a), (d). Increase: (e). Decrease: (b), (c).

Q10.24 Type 2 (it depends on velocity).

Q10.25 In practice, no—since the worker is free to deviate from the "required" dependence of force on position. (But in principle, yes—if the worker flawlessly performs according to the specifications.)

Q10.26 The speed is zero at x_1 and x_5, has a minimum at x_3, and has maxima at x_2 and x_4.

Q10.27 (a) The motion is confined to a region near x_2 or a region near x_4. (b) The particle is unconfined and will move off toward $x = +\infty$.

Q10.28 By a vertical line. By a steeply sloping line.

Q10.29 (1) By a single point at negative E $(0 > E > U)$. [The point is at $E = \frac{1}{2}U$.] (2) By a horizontal line segment at negative E that reaches neither the earth's radius nor the potential-energy curve.

Q10.30 No significant advantage from decreased gravity. Possibly a significant advantage from decreased air resistance.

Q10.31 [In the context of this chapter, the student should point out that the force acting between the wheel and the surface on which it rolls does no work (or almost no work) because the wheel is motionless at its point of contact with the surface. (See also Problem 10.18.)]

Q10.32 Sphere, cylinder, hoop.

Q10.33 Mass plays no role because both bodies are accelerated by gravity. They acquire the same total kinetic energy per unit mass. For the cylinder, only some of this kinetic energy is translational. For the block, it is all translational.

Q10.34 Yes.

Q10.35 The torque is independent of the angular speed.

Q10.37 Friction is an example. When friction acts, total energy is still conserved, but mechanical energy is not.

Q10.38 It appears as added internal energy of the acid bath (manifested—in principle—by a higher final temperature of the acid bath).

. . . .

E10.1 (At 3,000 food calories per day, the energy supplied to a person in a year by the food that he eats is about 4.6×10^{9} J, or 1,270 kW hr.)

E10.2 About 16 sec.

E10.3 (a) 0.0209 eV. (b) 1.902 eV. (c) 4.69×10^{6} eV, or 4.69 MeV. (d) 3.12×10^{8} eV, or 312 MeV.

E10.4 (1) 29.8 kilotons. (2) Yes. (The vessel could be given a speed of 9.17×10^{4} m/sec, more than 8 times escape speed.)

E10.5 (1) 1.578×10^{15} J. (2) 0.0527 kg, or 52.7 gm. (3) The same as at the nuclear station.

E10.6 (1) 3.91×10^{26} J/sec. (2) 4.35×10^{9} kg/sec. (3) 1.375×10^{15} sec, or 4.36×10^{7} years.

E10.7 (3) Equation 10.1 is applicable and $\mathbf{s} = 0$.

E10.8 (a) $mg\ell$. (b) $-mg\ell$. (The answers are independent of v_0.)

E10.9 (a) $-mgh$. (b) mgh. (c) Zero. (The answers are independent of s.)

E10.10 (1) - 41 J. (2) Zero.

E10.11 (1)(a) $2aF_0$. (b) $2aF_0$. (c) $-2aF_0$. (d) Zero. (2) $2aF_0$, the same as in a straight-line displacement from 0,0 to a,a.

E10.12 (a) 3.40×10^5 J (mgd sin 10 deg).
(b) $- 3.40 \times 10^5$ J. (c) Zero.

E10.13 (a) 1 m/sec. (b) 2.5 m. (c) 500 J. (d) 500 J.

E10.14 $2v_1^2/g$.

E10.15 (1) 3×10^7 m/sec. (2) 2×10^{-14} N. (3) 4×10^{-10} N, greater than the electron's weight by a factor of 4.5×10^{19}.

E10.16 Yes, it is approximately valid in practice.

E10.17 (1) $\underline{A}$ is the force exerted by the air on the spacecraft (or by the craft on the air). It is the energy per unit distance transferred from the craft to the air. (2) K depends quadratically on t: $K = K_o - A[v_o t - \frac{1}{2}(A/m)t^2]$, where $v_o = \sqrt{2K_o/m}$. (3) The acceleration is constant (its magnitude is A/m).

E10.18 (1) $s \sim v_o$. (2) $\text{Cost} \sim s^2$.

E10.19 Work by gravity = $- 2.64 \times 10^4$ J. Work by elevator = $+ 3.12 \times 10^4$ J. Since the man's kinetic energy is zero at the 1st and 14th floors, the <u>total</u> work done on him by gravity plus the elevator is zero during the ascent.

E10.20 (2) K_o is minimum at $\theta = 45$ deg. (It approaches infinity at $\theta = 0$ and $\frac{1}{2}\pi$.)

E10.21 (2) $- \frac{1}{2}kx_1^2$. It is the work done by the applied force as the body moves from 0 to x_1.

E10.22 $W_A = \beta a^2$. $W_B = 0$. No, it cannot be the only force. <u>Optional</u>: $W_C = \frac{1}{2}\beta a^2$.

E10.23 - 2 J.

E10.24 (2) Unlikely. (From A to B, the work done by gravity was 196 J/kg and the gain of kinetic energy was 182 J/kg, so the energy dissipated through friction was 14 J/kg. At B the car has a kinetic energy of 200 J/kg. Since it lost 14 J/kg rolling downhill, it is likely to lose more than 4 J/kg rolling uphill, which will prevent its reaching point D.)

E10.25 (1) Zero. (2) Zero. (3) 2mgh. (4) 2mgh.

E10.26 (The energy of the more massive body may often be ignored. In the center-of-mass frame, the two bodies have equal magnitudes of momentum but the lighter body has most of the kinetic energy.)

E10.27 (1) Harmonic oscillation relative to a uniformly moving center of mass. (2) $K = mv_c^2 + mv_0^2 \cos^2 \omega t$. The first term is the translational part of the kinetic energy; the second term is the internal part. (3) $\mu = \frac{1}{2}m$. The effective single body executes simple harmonic motion. Its velocity is $v = -2v_0 \cos \omega t$. (The position of the effective single body is $x = s_0 - (2v_0/\omega) \sin \omega t$, where s_0 is the equilibrium length of the spring.)

E10.28 1,176 W.

E10.29 $P = 4.2 \times 10^4$ W = 42 kW = 56 horsepower. (a) Comparable to the power delivered by an automobile engine. (b) More than the typical electric power consumption in a home.

E10.31 20 N.

E10.32 (1) $(\ell_1 + \ell_2)/\ell_2$. (2) $[(\ell_1 + \ell_2)/\ell_2]^2$.

E10.33 $r_1 r_3/r_2 r_4$.

E10.34 (A simple method is to note that pulling the free end of the rope through a distance ℓ raises the lower hook through a distance $\frac{1}{4}\ell$.)

E10.35 (1) 306 N. (Idealized M.A. = 30; actual M.A. = 24.) (2) (a) Barely (98 percent of the child's weight is required). (b) Yes. (c) Yes.

E10.36 (1) M.A. = $2\pi R/d$. (2) $\pi R/d$.

E10.37 (Both methods give $K = mgy$. Method 2 is substantially simpler.)

E10.38 (1) 5.99×10^4 J. (2) 4.08 m.

E10.39 (1) 1.84×10^4 m, or 18.4 km. (2) 1.02×10^4 m, or 10.2 km.

E10.40 (a) 9.8 J. (b) 2.2 J. (c) 12 J.

E10.41 (1) − 0.531 J. (2) − 0.735 J. (Energies and energy changes—all in joules—are $K_1 = 5.400$, $K_2 = 4.134$, $\Delta K = -1.266$, $\Delta U = +0.735$, $\Delta E = -0.531$.)

E10.42 $\frac{1}{2}m(v_x^2 + v_y^2) + mgy + U_0 = E =$ constant. One adjustable constant. (2) No.

E10.43 (2) $v_{top}/v_0 = \cos\theta$.

E10.44 (1) 198 m/sec. (2) Going up: $U = mgy$, $K \cong 0$ ($E \cong mgy$). Coming down: $U = mgy$, $K = 2mg(y_{max} - y)$ ($E = mg(2y_{max} - y)$). The rocket thrust is a non-conservative force whose effect is not included in the potential energy.

E10.45 (1) $U = eE(x - x_0)$. (2) Yes.

E10.46 (1) $U = \frac{1}{2}k_1x^2 - \frac{1}{4}k_2x^4$. (2) Zero. (3) $\frac{1}{4}(k_1^2/k_2)$.

E10.47 (1) $F_x = -k(x - a) - mg$. (2) At $x = a - (mg/k)$. There $U = -\frac{1}{2}(m^2g^2/k)$, $K = E + \frac{1}{2}(m^2g^2/k)$.

E10.48 (1) (One method: Set $n = t/T$ and write $0.99 = e^{-0.01}$. Then $E_n = E(t) = (e^{-0.01})^{t/T}E_0 = E_0e^{-t/100T}$. Another method, equivalent to the first: Take logarithms and write $\ln E = n \ln 0.99 + \ln E_0 = -0.01n + \ln E_0$, or $\ln (E/E_0) = -0.01t/T$. This leads to the same result.)
(2) $(E_0/\tau)e^{-t/\tau}$.

E10.49 (1) $v_0 = \sqrt{\frac{1}{2}gh}$. (2)

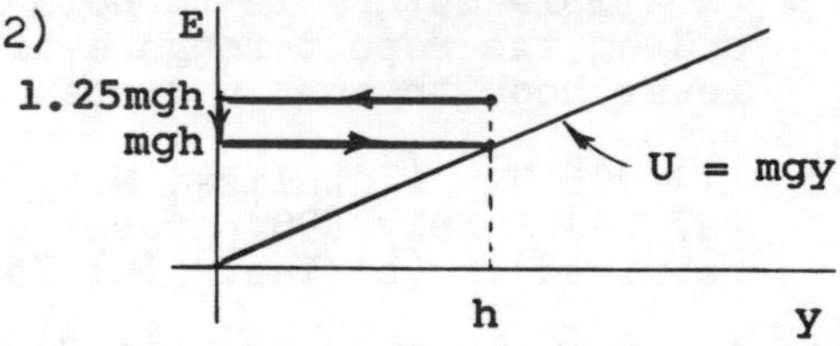

E10.50 (In a frame of reference moving with the racket, the speed of the ball is at most $v_0 + v_1$ before the collision (for perpendicular incidence) and at most $v_0 + v_1$ after the collision (for an elastic collision), so the ball's speed after the collision is at most $v_0 + 2v_1$ in the earth-fixed frame of reference.)

E10.51 $E = \frac{1}{2}mv_0^2 + mgz_0$.

E10.52 (1) 2.00×10^{-11} m, or 0.2 Å. (2)(a) 2,830 m/sec. (b) 4.00×10^{17} m/sec^2. (3) Maximum speed at $x = 0$. Maximum acceleration at $x = \pm 0.2$ Å.

E10.53 (1)

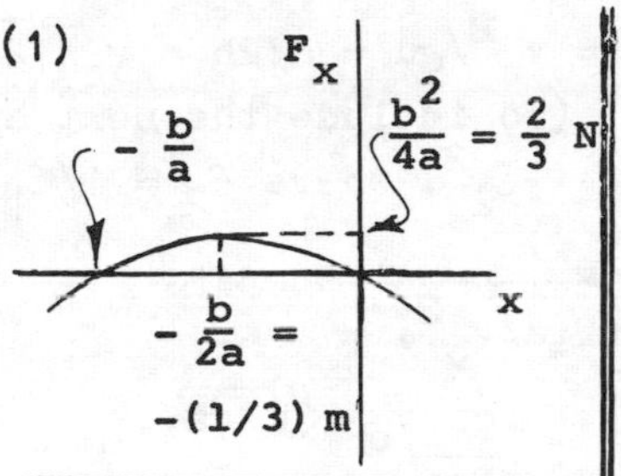

(2) $U = (1/3)ax^3 + \frac{1}{2}bx^2$.

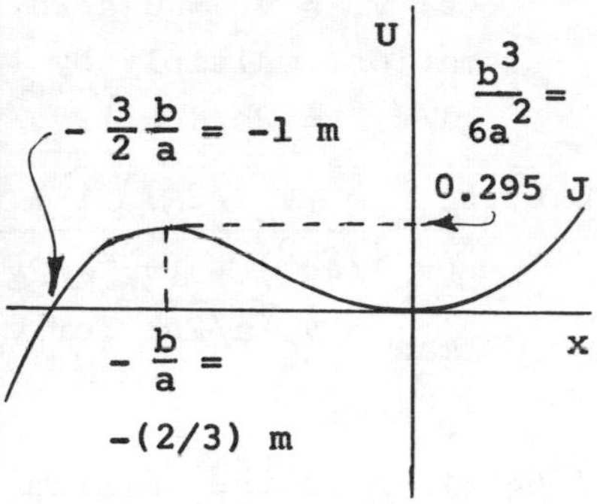

(4) $|x| \leqslant 0.1$ m.
$|x| \leqslant 0.01$ m.

E10.54 (1)

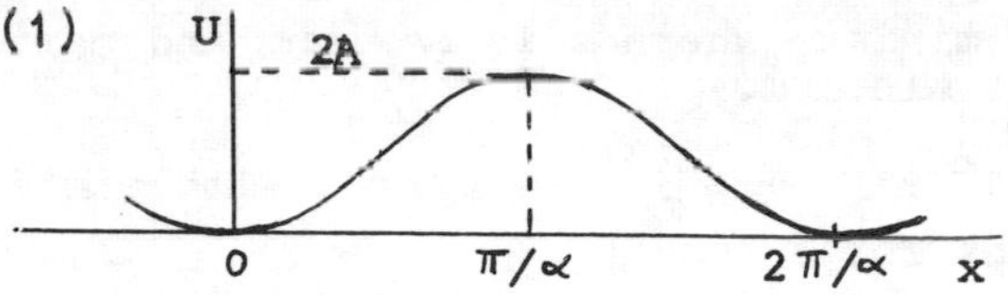

(2) $k = A\alpha^2$.
(3) $\omega = \alpha\sqrt{A/m}$.

E10.55 $v_f = \sqrt{2gR} = 1.12 \times 10^4$ m/sec. 1.34×10^7 sec, or 0.424 year, or 155 days.

E10.56 2.38×10^3 m/sec. About $7v_{sound}$.

E10.57 $I = m_1r_1{}^2 + m_2r_2{}^2 = \mu r^2$ (μ = reduced mass, r = distance between bodies). ($K = \frac{1}{2}I\omega^2 = \frac{1}{2}\mu v^2$, where v = relative speed.)

E10.58 $\frac{1}{2}mg \sin\theta$.

E10.60 $a = \left(\frac{M + 4m}{M + 6m}\right)g \sin\theta$. For $M \gg 4m$, $a \cong g \sin\theta$; for $M \ll 4m$, $a \cong (2/3)g \sin\theta$.

E10.61 (1) 4.48×10^4 W, or 60 horsepower.
(2) By about 17 percent (from 214 N m to 178 N m).

E10.62 (1) v_1 can be written as a function of d and any 2 of the 3 quantities v_0, g, and h:
$v_1 = v_0\sqrt{1 + (gd/v_0{}^2)^2} = v_0\sqrt{1 + (2h/d)^2} = \sqrt{2gh}\sqrt{1 + (d/2h)^2}$. (2)(a) $v_1 \cong gd/v_0 = (2h/d)v_0 = \sqrt{2gh}$. (To include the next approximation, multiply

by $1 + \frac{1}{2}\mathcal{E}_1^{\,2}$, where $\mathcal{E}_1 = v_0^{\,2}/gd = d/2h = v_0/\sqrt{2gh}$.)
(b) $v_1 \cong v_0 = d\sqrt{g/2h}$. (To include the next approximation, multiply by $1 + \frac{1}{2}\mathcal{E}_2^{\,2}$, where $\mathcal{E}_2 = 1/\mathcal{E}_1 = gd/v_0^{\,2} = 2h/d = \sqrt{2gh}/v_0$.)

E10.63 $s_{max} = (v_0^{\,2}/2g)\sqrt{1 + (2ga/v_0^{\,2})} = \sqrt{(v_0^{\,4}/4g^2) + (v_0^{\,2}a/2g)}$. For $v_0 \ll \sqrt{2ga}$, $s_{max} \cong x_{max} = v_0\sqrt{a/2g}$; for $v_0 \gg \sqrt{2ga}$, $s_{max} \cong y_{max} = v_0^{\,2}/2g$.

E10.64 (1) <u>h</u> is the maximum vertical height of the track. <u>a</u> is the horizontal distance between successive troughs (or crests) of the track.
(2) $v = \sqrt{v_0^{\,2} + gh[1 - \sin(\pi x/a)]}$.
(3) (<u>v</u> is minimum where z is maximum and maximum where z is minimum.)

E10.65 $F_x = Cx/(x^2 + y^2 + z^2)^{3/2} = Cx/r^3$, with similar expressions for F_y and F_z.

E10.66 (2) $\frac{1}{4}mgR$ (or $\frac{1}{4}GmM_E/R$). (3) $v_2 = \sqrt{gR}$ (or $\sqrt{GM_E/R}$).

E10.67 (1) $E = \frac{1}{2}mv^2 + mg\ell(1 - \cos\theta)$,
or $E = \frac{1}{2}m(ds/dt)^2 + mg\ell[1 - \cos(s/\ell)]$,
or $E = \frac{1}{2}m(v_x^{\,2} + v_y^{\,2}) + mgy$ (s, ℓ, and θ are defined in Figure 10.28; x and <u>y</u> are horizontal and vertical coordinates of the bob).
(2)

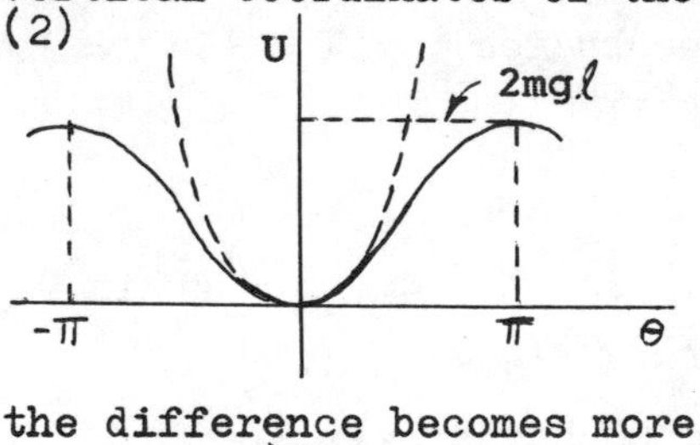

(3) (The explanation should make use of the fact that the actual restoring force (slope of the solid curve) is less than the restoring force of a harmonic oscillator (slope of the dashed parabola); the difference becomes more significant as θ increases.)

E10.68 Brenda is right. ($\ell = v_0^{\,2}/g\theta^2$, where v_0 = 10/45 m/sec.)

. . . .

P10.1 Valid if $W \ll mv^2$ or $\Delta v \ll v$.

P10.2 (1) (Write $K = \frac{1}{2}m\mathbf{v}\cdot\mathbf{v}$ and differentiate with respect to time.) (2) It is the rate at which the force $\mathbf{F}'$ is adding energy to the particle.

P10.3 (1) It moves in one dimension along the x axis, oscillating indefinitely between end points at $x = 0$ and $x = \frac{1}{2}\ell$. Its maximum kinetic energy, $\ell F_0/2\pi$, is achieved at $x = \frac{1}{4}\ell$. (2) At $x = \frac{1}{2}\ell$.

P10.4 (a) $\mathbf{r}_c = \frac{1}{2}a\mathbf{i} + (3/4)a\mathbf{j}$. (b) $\mathbf{r}_1' = -\frac{1}{2}a\mathbf{i} - (3/4)a\mathbf{j}$, $\mathbf{r}_2' = -\frac{1}{2}a\mathbf{i} + \frac{1}{4}a\mathbf{j}$, $\mathbf{r}_3' = \frac{1}{2}a\mathbf{i} + \frac{1}{4}a\mathbf{j}$. (c) $\mathbf{v}_3 = \frac{1}{2}v_0\mathbf{i} - (3/2)v_0\mathbf{j}$. (d) $\mathbf{v}_1' = 2v_0\mathbf{i}$, $\mathbf{v}_2' = -v_0\mathbf{i} + 3v_0\mathbf{j}$, $\mathbf{v}_3' = -\frac{1}{2}v_0\mathbf{i} - (3/2)v_0\mathbf{j}$. (e) $2mv_0^2$. (f) $9.5\ mv_0^2$.

P10.5 $a = (F_1/m)(L_1/L_2) - g = (L_1/L_2)[(F_1 - F_0)/m]$, where F_0 is the applied force (acting downward) that just suffices to balance the load, and F_1 is the actual applied force. $K = [F_1(L_1/L_2) - mg]d_2 = [F_1 - mg(L_2/L_1)]d_1 = (L_1/L_2)(F_1 - F_0)d_2 = (F_1 - F_0)/d_1$. ($L_1$, L_2, d_1, and d_2 are defined in Figure 10.12.)

P10.6 (1) 705 J. (2) 235 J by the man lifting the corner, 470 J by the man lifting the side.

P10.7 (1) (The square root in the denominator is v_x. For $x_1 < x_2$, take the positive square root ($v_x > 0$); for $x_1 > x_2$, take the negative square root ($v_x < 0$).)

P10.8 ($T = 2\pi\sqrt{m/k}$.)

P10.9 $T = 4\sqrt{2mE}/K$.

P10.10 (3) (Argument to accompany method 1: Equation 10.93 satisfies Equation 10.92 only if $\omega = \sqrt{k/m}$ and $A = \sqrt{2E/k}$; therefore ω and A are not independent of the other quantities. Argument to accompany method 2: Equation 10.92 contains one arbitrary constant (E). It is integrated once, which introduces a second arbitrary constant (φ).)

P10.11 (1) $E > 0$: Unbounded motion; the speed is minimum ($v_{min} = \sqrt{2E/m}$) at $x = 0$. $E = 0$: See part 2. $E < 0$: Motion unbounded but confined to $x > x_0$ or $x < -x_0$, where $x_0 = \sqrt{2|E|/k}$. In all cases, speed and kinetic energy become infinite as $x \to \pm\infty$. (2) $\frac{1}{2}m(dx/dt)^2 - \frac{1}{2}kx^2 = E = 0$. $x(t) = x_0e^{\pm\alpha t}$, where $\alpha = \sqrt{k/m}$. At $t = 0$, the object is at x_0 (which may be positive or negative). For the choice of positive exponent, the object is initially moving away from the origin; it continues with rapidly increasing acceleration to infinite distance. For the choice of negative exponent, the object is initially moving toward the origin; it decelerates and needs an infinite time to reach the origin.

P10.12 $C = -mgR$. <u>Optional</u>: $U = -mgR + mg(r - R) - (mg/R)(r - R)^2 + (mg/R^2)(r - R)^3 - \ldots$.

P10.13 [Note: In early printings of the text, the potential-energy function is given as $U = A(e^{\alpha x} + e^{-\alpha x} - 1)$. It should be $U = A(e^{\alpha x} + e^{-\alpha x} - 2)$.] (1) $U \cong \alpha^2 A x^2$; $k = 2\alpha^2 A$, $a = 0$. (2) 2.09 sec. 0.0667 m. (3) For small energy, $U(x)$ is approximately parabolic (a harmonic-oscillator potential), so the period is nearly independent of amplitude. For larger energy and larger amplitude, $U(x)$ rises <u>faster</u> than a harmonic-oscillator potential. The restoring force is therefore <u>greater</u> than for a harmonic-oscillator and the period decreases.

P10.14 (1) $U(r) = \frac{2Ze^2}{4\pi\varepsilon_0}\frac{1}{r}$. (2)

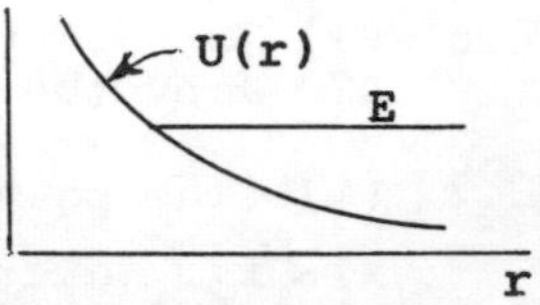

(3) $r_{min} = \frac{2Ze^2}{4\pi\varepsilon_0 E}$.

2.28×10^{-13} m (228 fm, or 2.28×10^{-3} Å). [Note the convenient factor $e^2/4\pi\varepsilon_0$ given on page A10.]

P10.15 (1) $\sqrt{5ga}$. (2) 4mg. [Mechanical energy is conserved and the <u>total</u> force is mv^2/a at all points around the circle.]

P10.16 (1) No. (2) No. (3) Yes, $\ell_0 = 4.945$ m.

P10.17 (1) $\mathbf{L}_{orbital} = \mathbf{L}_{spin} = MR^2\omega\mathbf{k}$, where $\mathbf{k}$ is a unit vector directed into the page in Figure 10.22; $\mathbf{L}_{total} = 2MR^2\omega\mathbf{k}$. (2) $MgR \sin\theta\, \mathbf{k}$.
(3) $\alpha = (g/2R) \sin\theta$, $a_c = \frac{1}{2}g \sin\theta$.

P10.18 (1) (The wheel is motionless at its point of contact with the surface; $d\mathbf{s} = 0$ and $dW = \mathbf{F}_f \cdot d\mathbf{s} = 0$.)
(3) $\frac{1}{2}m(dx_c/dt)^2[1 + (k/r)^2] - K_0 = Fx_c[1 + (b/r)]$.

P10.19 (1) $v_c = \sqrt{\dfrac{2g(z_0 - z)}{1 + (I/mb^2)}}$, $\omega = \dfrac{v_c}{b} = \sqrt{\dfrac{2g(z_0 - z)}{b^2 + (I/m)}}$.

(If the radius of gyration is used, I/mb^2 is replaced by k^2/b^2 and I/m by k^2.)
(2) $a_c = g/[1 + (I/mb^2)]$. (3)(a) $a_c/g = 1/51 = 0.0196$. (b) 50.

P10.20 ($K = \frac{1}{2}I\omega^2 = \frac{1}{4}MR^2(d\theta/dt)^2$, $U = Mgh = Mgr_c(1 - \cos\theta) \cong (2/3\pi)MgR\theta^2$.)

P10.21 (Write $\frac{1}{2}mv_1{}^2 - (C/r_1) = \frac{1}{2}mv_2{}^2 - (C/r_2)$ and $r_1v_1 = r_2v_2$. Solve these equations simultaneously to find $\frac{1}{2}mv_1{}^2 = Cr_2/[r_1(r_1 + r_2)]$ and $E = -C/(r_1 + r_2)$.)

P10.23 $\mathbf{v}_1 = \frac{1}{2}v\mathbf{i} + \frac{1}{2}v\mathbf{j}$, $\mathbf{v}_2 = \frac{1}{2}v\mathbf{i} - \frac{1}{2}v\mathbf{j}$. (Both speeds are $v/\sqrt{2}$; the velocities are perpendicular.)

P10.24 (1) (A simple method: Square the momentum-conservation equation, $\mathbf{p}_1 + \mathbf{p}_2 = \mathbf{p}_0$; this gives $p_1{}^2 + 2\mathbf{p}_1 \cdot \mathbf{p}_2 + p_2{}^2 = p_0{}^2$. Since energy conservation requires that $p_1{}^2 + p_2{}^2 = p_0{}^2$, the scalar product $\mathbf{p}_1 \cdot \mathbf{p}_2$ must be zero.)
(2) If either final velocity is zero, the other final velocity is equal to the velocity of the incident particle.

P10.25 (1) $\frac{1}{2}m_1v_1{}^2 + \frac{1}{2}m_2v_2{}^2 = \frac{1}{2}m_1v_0{}^2$, or

$$\frac{v_2{}^2}{(m_1/m_2)v_0{}^2} + \frac{v_1{}^2}{v_0{}^2} = 1.$$

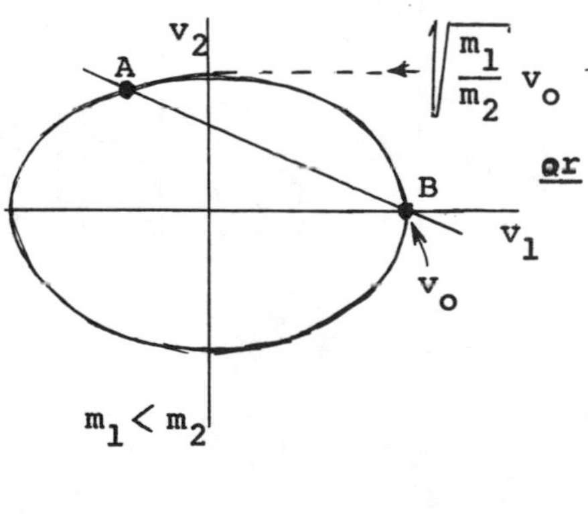

or

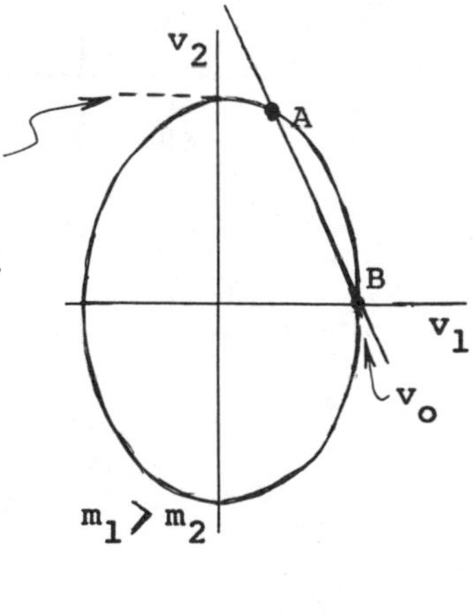

(2) An ellipse. (3) Two intersection points. For impenetrable balls, point A ($v_2 > 0$) is acceptable.

(4) $v_1 = \left(\frac{m_1 - m_2}{m_1 + m_2}\right) v_o$, $v_2 = \left(\frac{2m_1}{m_1 + m_2}\right) v_o$.

P10.26 (1)

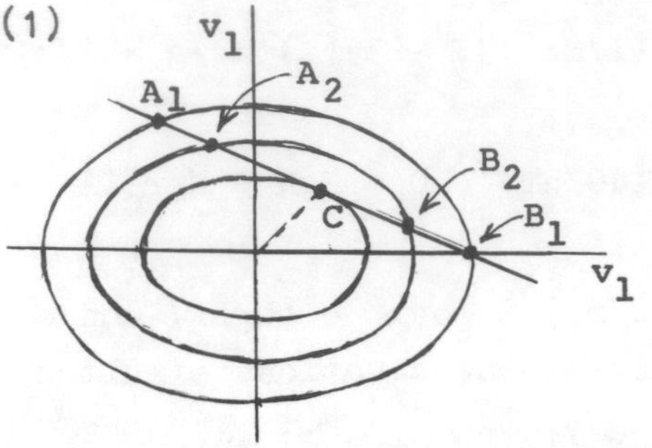

A_1: acceptable elastic solution (for $m_1 < m_2$).

A_2: acceptable inelastic solution.

C : Solution for minimum "inelasticity factor" γ.

(2) The linear dimensions of the energy ellipse are proportional to $\sqrt{\gamma}$. $\gamma_{min} = m_1/(m_1 + m_2)$.

(3) The energy ellipse and the momentum line are tangent. $v_1 = v_2 = [m_1/(m_1 + m_2)] v_o$. The balls stick together and move as a unit after the collision.

P10.27 (2) All of the energy of ball 2 goes to ball 5. All of the energy of ball 1 goes to ball 4. Therefore balls 5 and 4 swing out in rapid succession to reach the same angle, equal to the initial angle of balls 1 and 2. (3) Balls 1 and 2 will swing out with 8/9 of the initial energy of ball 5 (2/3 of its initial speed). Ball 5 will rebound with 1/9 of its initial energy (1/3 of its initial speed). Balls 3 and 4 will remain motionless.

(4) The following table shows the velocities of the balls before the first collision and after each successive collision.

1 and 2	3	4	5
v	0	0	0
(1/3)v	(4/3)v	0	0
(1/3)v	0	(4/3)v	0
(1/3)v	0	0	(4/3)v
(1/9)v	(4/9)v	0	(4/3)v
(1/9)v	0	(4/9)v	(4/3)v
(1/27)v	(4/27)v	(4/9)v	(4/3)v

CHAPTER 11

Q11.2 (Visual observation of the earth, sun, and planets, for example.)

Q11.3 (a) $m^3/kg\ sec^2$. (b) $J\ m/kg^2$.

Q11.5 No, because the object and the earth are both equally accelerated by the sun. (The side of the earth away from the sun is falling "downward;" the side of the earth nearer the sun is falling "upward.") [See also Problem 11.29.]

Q11.6 The method defines gravitational mass. (For example: Use a balance to identify two objects of equal mass. Measure the gravitational force between these two objects when they are a known distance apart. The mass of one of them is then $m = \sqrt{Fr^2/G}$.) [In the method of this example, G is an arbitrary constant rather than a measured quantity. A variation of the method that makes use of a standard kilogram is possible; then G would be an experimentally determined quantity.]

Q11.7 (a) No. (b) Yes.

Q11.8 1. Man on the moon (mg/6). 2. Man on the tower (mg/2.25). 3. Man in the shaft (mg/2). 4. Man on the earth's surface (mg).

Q11.9 F(r) rises more steeply near r = 0 and less steeply near r = R. Its graph has negative curvature (it is concave downward).

Q11.10 (2) Its total energy. (This is the main reason that a discontinuity in U is inconvenient.)

Q11.11

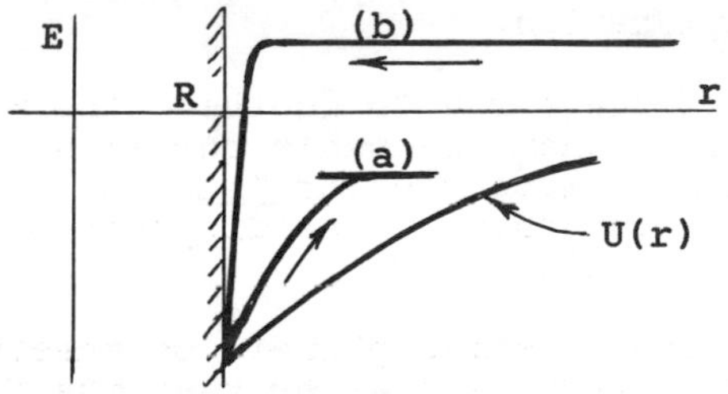

Q11.12 They are equally likely to escape. They have equal total energy.

Q11.16 His scale is probably a balance that compares one weight with another. The comparison weights and the weight of coffee increase by the same factor.

Q11.17 (If the last quoted digits are accurate, the uncertainty in g is less than 10 ppm. Note that $g \sim \ell/T^2$.)

Q11.19 (1) Zero. (2) It is a straight-line segment.

Q11.20 Calculate its energy per unit mass, $E/m = -(GM_S/r) + \frac{1}{2}v^2$. Its orbit is elliptic if $E/m < 0$, parabolic if $E/m = 0$, and hyperbolic if $E/m > 0$.

Q11.22 The eccentricity of its elliptical orbit may decrease, causing its average distance from the earth to decrease. The resulting decrease of its average <u>potential</u> energy will be greater than its decrease of <u>total</u> energy, so its average kinetic energy will increase. [In an inverse-square force field, $\overline{K} = -\frac{1}{2}\overline{U} = -E$. If the magnitude of decrease of energy is ΔE, $\overline{U}$ decreases by $2\Delta E$ and $\overline{K}$ increases by ΔE. (Incidentally, the fractional decrease of semimajor axis is the same as the fractional decrease of energy.)]

Q11.24 (1) A pair of exhaust jets can provide a couple (zero force and nonzero torque). (2) At apogee.

Q11.25 Yes. The orbits are as shown. Given enough time, the two craft should be close together again.

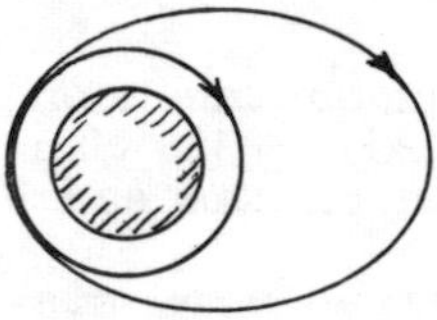

Q11.26 Yes, with respect to <u>any</u> fixed point.

Q11.27 Kepler's second law (the law of areas).

Q11.29 Mercury and Venus. The heliocentric theory offers the simpler explanation.

Q11.31 From one part of the earth to another, the moon's force changes more than the sun's force; a few thousand miles is a much greater fraction of the distance to the moon than of the distance to the sun. [See also Problem 11.29.]

Q11.32 Jupiter is the most massive planet, so massive that its force on the earth is greater than the force of the nearer planets.

. . . .

E11.1 (1) 7.97×10^3 N. (2) 7.97×10^3 N. (3) 3.99 m/sec^2. (4) 1.33×10^{-21} m/sec^2.

E11.2 (1) $F = 2.50 \times 10^{-6}$ N. $F/mg = 3.40 \times 10^{-9}$.
(2) The force of the breeze is much greater.

Reasonable range for F(breeze)/F(car): 10^4 to 10^7. [The student wanting to check or improve his or her estimate can be referred ahead to Equation 12.67. With $C_D = 1$, $A = 0.6$ m^2, $\rho = 1$ kg/m^3, and $v = 1$ m/sec (2 mile/hr), F(breeze) = 0.3 N, which makes F(breeze)/F(car) $\cong 10^5$. Suggestion: Refer the student ahead <u>after</u> he or she has completed this exercise, not before.]

E11.3 $\mathbf{F}_{21} = -Gm_1m_2\mathbf{r}_{21}/(r_{21})^3$.

E11.4 2.26×10^{39}. Gravity can be ignored in considering atomic structure.

E11.5 $F_{sun}/F_{earth} \cong 6 \times 10^{-4}$; $F_{moon}/F_{earth} \cong 3 \times 10^{-6}$; $F_{Venus}/F_{earth} \cong 10^{-9}$ (from 2×10^{-8} at shortest distance to 5×10^{-10} at greatest distance).

E11.7 Sample calculations:

Mass		(1)	(2)	(3)	
110 lb	49.9 kg	489 N	122 N	27,700 miles	4.46×10^7 m
140 lb	63.5 kg	622 N	156 N	31,200 miles	5.03×10^7 m
170 lb	77.1 kg	756 N	189 N	34,400 miles	5.54×10^7 m
200 lb	90.7 kg	889 N	222 N	37,300 miles	6.01×10^7 m

E11.8 $a_0 = 7.41 \times 10^{-10}$ m/sec^2. Approximately 1 day (an upper limit is $\sqrt{2s/a_0} = 90{,}000$ sec = 25 hr). No danger of starving. [See also Problem 11.2.]

E11.10 (1)(a) $T \sim r^{-\frac{1}{2}}$, where r is the distance from the center of the earth. (b) $T \sim r$. (2) 78 miles (1.26×10^5 m) downward; 39.6 miles (6.37×10^4 m) upward. <u>Optional</u>: (Air pressure changes by 1 percent in 80 m; this is 800 times the fractional rate of change of a pendulum's period. The barometer is much better suited than a pendulum for everyday measurements of altitude in the lower part of the atmosphere.)

E11.11 (1)(a) $v_z = v_0 \cos(\omega t + \varphi)$, where $\omega = \sqrt{g/R}$ $= \sqrt{GM_E/R^3}$ and $v_0 = A\omega$; A is the amplitude ($A \leqslant R$).

For the special case $A = R$, see part 2.
(b) $v_z = \sqrt{v_0^2 - \omega^2 z^2} = \omega\sqrt{A^2 - z^2}$. For the special case $A = R$, $v_z = \omega\sqrt{R^2 - z^2} = \sqrt{gR}\,\sqrt{1 - (z/R)^2}$ $= \sqrt{GM_E/R}\,\sqrt{1 - (z/R)^2}$. (2) $v_0 = A\sqrt{g/R} = A\sqrt{GM_E/R^3}$. For $A = R$, $v_0 = \sqrt{gR} = \sqrt{GM_E/R} = 7{,}910$ m/sec.

E11.12 (1) (For example, use a formula of constant acceleration, $s = \frac{1}{2}at^2$, for each half of a trip. The actual acceleration is $g \sin(7\ \text{deg}) = 1.19$ m/sec^2 at one end and zero at the center. Picking $a = 0.6$ m/sec^2 as an average gives 55 min for the travel time. Since the train spends more time near the ends than near the center, the average acceleration is actually greater than 0.6 m/sec^2. Picking $a = 1$ m/sec^2 gives 42 min.) (2) (The exact answer is 965 m/sec. Estimates in the range 700 m/sec to 1,400 m/sec are reasonable.)

E11.13 (1) 90 percent of the way from the center of the earth to the center of the moon: 3.46×10^8 m, or 2.15×10^5 miles, from the center of the earth; 3.84×10^7 m, or 2.38×10^4 miles, from the center of the moon. (2) Negative. (The contributions of both the earth and the moon are negative.)

E11.14 (a) $\frac{1}{2}mgR$, or $GmM_E/2R$. (b) $(3/2)mgR$, or $3GmM_E/2R$.

E11.15 (1) $r = GM_E/c^2 = 4.44 \times 10^{-3}$ m $= 4.44$ mm.
(2) 1,477 m, or 1.477 km.

E11.16

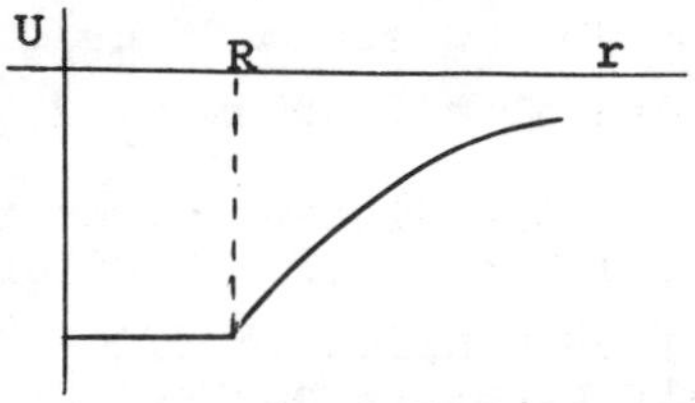

$r \leqslant R$: $U = -\dfrac{GmM}{R}$.

$r \geqslant R$: $U = -\dfrac{GmM}{r}$.

E11.17 (1)(a) $v = R\sqrt{g/r}$. (b) $v = \sqrt{GM_E/r}$.
(2) 3.66×10^9 m, or 2.27×10^6 miles.

E11.18 (This can be done without calculation by noting that the work required to put a satellite into a low earth orbit is half the escape energy, i.e. half the work needed to send the satellite to infinite distance.)

E11.19 (1) (Energy of circling satellite = $0.99E_o$; energy of vertically fired satellite = $0.98E_o$, where $E_o = mgR = GmM_E/R$ (the escape energy).)
(2) (Energy of circling satellite $\cong 0.50E_o$; energy of vertically fired satellite = $0.025E_o$.)

E11.20 r(from center of earth) = 50.25R = 199,000 miles = 3.20×10^8 m. h(from surface) = 49.25R = 195,000 miles = 3.14×10^8 m.

E11.21 (1) $E \cong GmM_E\left(\frac{1}{R} - \frac{1}{r}\right) = 0.98\,\frac{GmM_E}{R}$.
(2) $E \cong -GmM_E/r = -0.02GmM_E/R$.
(3) $v \cong \sqrt{1.96GM_E/R} = 1.11 \times 10^4$ m/sec. (Note that this is approximately v_{esc}.)

E11.22 (1) 2.38×10^3 m/sec. (2) 4.71 ($= \sqrt{(M_E/M_M)(R_M/R_E)}$).

E11.23 (1) R_1/R_2. (2) $\sqrt{M_1/M_2}$.

E11.24 (1) No. $v_{esc}(\text{asteroid}) = 10^{-3}v_{esc}(\text{earth}) \cong$ 11 m/sec (= 25 mile/hr). Jumping vertically in a negligible gravitational field, a man could probably not achieve a speed greater than 5 or 6 m/sec. [This conclusion can be reached in several ways, and students should be encouraged to do experiments or make observations to validate their conclusions. Here are three approaches: 1. Jump vertically on earth and determine the maximum "takeoff" speed (about 3 m/sec). Estimate what fraction of the body's output energy goes into kinetic energy and what fraction into potential energy before leaving the ground. Assume that all this energy would go into kinetic energy on the asteroid; then estimate the takeoff speed on the asteroid (about 5 m/sec). 2. Consider the nearly horizontal "jump" of a racing swimmer as he leaves the starting platform. The initial horizontal velocity that he can give himself on earth is comparable to the initial vertical velocity that he could give himself on the asteroid. 3. Note that the maximum speed of a sprinter is about 10 m/sec. He cannot achieve this speed in a single push off the starting blocks. At least several successive "pushes" (steps) are required.]
(2) Yes. $v_{orbit} \cong 8$ m/sec $\cong 18$ mile/hr, easily achieved with a thrown baseball. [Suggestion: Ask the student to justify his or her conclusion, either with the help of Equation 7.94 or with approximate measurements of baseball speeds.]

E11.25 He will drift away indefinitely. His speed exceeds the escape speed, which is 0.667 mm/sec. His total energy is positive.

E11.26 $v_{min} = \sqrt{2GM_E/r}$. For impulsive firing, $v_{min} \cong v_{esc}$. For $r \gg R$, $v_{min} \ll v_{esc}$.

E11.27 $v = (\sqrt{2} - 1)v = (\sqrt{2} - 1)\sqrt{GM_E/r}$. $\Delta v/v = \sqrt{2} - 1 = 0.414$.

E11.28 (1) $- GM_EM_S/r$. (2) $GM_EM_S/2r$. (3) $GM_EM_S/2r$.

E11.29 (1) 4.21×10^4 m/sec. (2) 1.414 (it is $\sqrt{2}$). (3) 3.77. (The energy requirement to reach Neptune is about $(3.77)^2$, or 14, times greater than the energy requirement to reach the moon.)

E11.30 (1) a = 16,400 miles, b = 11,050 miles, c = 12,120 miles. (2) 0.739.

E11.31 (1) 2,090 miles. (2) 4.46. (3) For a synchronous satellite ($T \cong 24$ hr), a = 26,200 miles (see page 236 of the text). For Intelstat 2A, a = 16,500 miles. From Kepler's third law, the ratio of the periods is $(26{,}200/16{,}500)^{3/2} = 2.00$.

E11.32 (2) Perihelion is at 0.6 A.U., between the orbits of Mercury and Venus. Aphelion is at 35.0 A.U., beyond the orbit of Neptune.

E11.34 2π.

E11.35 A hyperbola. The curves approach straight lines of slope ± 2 as $x^2 \to \infty$.

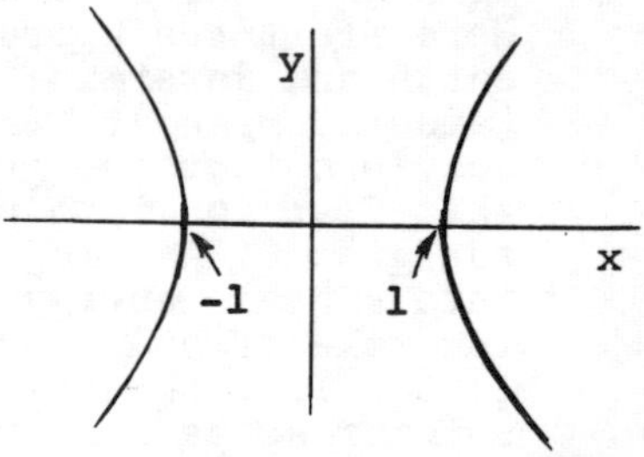

E11.36 57.9.

E11.37 0.0894 year.

E11.38 (a) 26,300 miles. (b) 88.4 min.

E11.39 [Note: r = 26,200 miles.] (1) 6.08 miles. (2) 4.33 mile/day.

E11.40 (1) 1.018. (2) 252 min, or 1.51×10^4 sec, or 4.20 hr. (3) Part 1 would be unchanged; it depends only on the conservation of angular momentum.

E11.41 $\kappa_S = 1.00\ (\text{year})^2/(\text{A.U.})^3$.

E11.42 (Use $\frac{M_S}{M_E} = \frac{(T^2/a^3)_{\text{satellite}}}{(T^2/a^3)_{\text{planet}}}$.)

E11.43 $v^2r = \gamma = \text{constant}$, or $v^2 = \gamma/r$, or $v = \sqrt{\gamma/r}$, where $\gamma = GM_S$.

E11.44 (1) 8×10^{10} N m. (2) 9.6×10^{12} kg m^2/sec. (3) $v_1 = 7.06 \times 10^3$ m/sec, $L_1 = 5.65 \times 10^{14}$ kg m^2/sec, $K_1 = 2.49 \times 10^{11}$ J. (4) $v_2 = 7.18 \times 10^3$ m/sec, $L_2 = 5.75 \times 10^{14}$ kg m^2/sec, $K_2 = 2.58 \times 10^{11}$ J. (5) It goes into an elliptical orbit with perigee at $r = 8 \times 10^6$ m. (6)(a) It would have gone into an elliptical orbit with apogee at $r = 8 \times 10^6$ m. (b) It would have gone into an elliptical orbit with perigee at $r < 8 \times 10^6$ m and apogee at $r > 8 \times 10^6$ m (and with a very slight increase in semimajor axis).

. . . .

[Note to instructors: Although Chapter 11 by itself is less demanding than the mechanics chapters that precede it, a number of the problems in Chapter 11 are quite challenging. Many of them require application of knowledge and skills acquired in studying the earlier chapters.]

P11.1 (2)(a) Radially outward. (b) Radially inward. (Both answers assume that the basic force between particles is attractive.)

P11.2 (1) $t = \frac{1}{2}\pi\sqrt{r_0^3/2GM}$, where r_0 is the initial separation distance and M is the mass of the table with its load. (2) $t_{\text{exact}} = 7.07 \times 10^4$ sec = 1,178 min = 19.63 hr. $t_{\text{approx}} = \sqrt{2r_0^3/GM} = (4/\pi)t_{\text{exact}}$ = 25.0 hr. (3) Most of the time is spent at low speed near the initial position, where the acceleration is GM/r_0^2.

P11.3 (1) (The force is approximately Gmm'/b^2, the time is approximately b/v, the impulse is approximately Gmm'/bv, which is the transverse component of momentum given to the boy. The deflection angle is

approximately $\Delta p/m'v$, or Gm/bv^2.)
(2) (Example: $m = 60$ kg, $b = 3$ m, $v = 5$ m/sec; $\theta \cong 5 \times 10^{-11}$ radian.)

P11.4 (1) $\underset{\sim}{I} = (2Gmm'/bv)\underset{\sim}{j}$, where $\underset{\sim}{j}$ is a unit vector directed from the boy toward the girl at his point of closest approach. (3) $\theta = -U(b)/K_o$, where $U(b) = -Gmm'/b$ and $K_o = \frac{1}{2}m'v^2$.

P11.5 (3) 0.8 percent. <u>Optional</u>: $a \cong g - (2g/R)h + (3g/R^2)h^2$.

P11.6 (1) $(2/\pi)\sqrt{gR}$, or $(2/\pi)\sqrt{GM_E/R}$. (2) $(\pi/4)\sqrt{gR}$, or $(\pi/4)\sqrt{GM_E/R}$. The orbital speed of a low-altitude satellite is $v_o = \sqrt{gR}$, the same as the speed of the oscillating object at the center of the earth. The two averages are $(2/\pi)v_o$ ($= 0.637v_o$) and $(\pi/4)v_o$ ($= 0.785v_o$).

P11.8 The force is mg at the surface and decreases approximately linearly to zero at a depth of 10 miles. If x is measured downward from the surface, the motion within the hole is given by $x = h(1 - \cos\omega t)$ and $v_x = h\omega \sin \omega t$, where $h = 10$ miles and $\omega = \sqrt{g/h} = \sqrt{GM_E/R^2h} = 0.0247\ \text{sec}^{-1}$. The time to fall through the 10-mile hole is $t = \pi/2\omega = 63.6$ sec; the speed of an object as it leaves the bottom of the hole is $v_o = h\omega = 397$ m/sec; the time it spends coasting at constant speed across the interior of the planet is 3.20×10^4 sec, or 8.89 hr.

P11.9 [See the related Problem 10.21.]

P11.10 (1) (Note that $v^2 = v_\parallel{}^2 + v_\perp{}^2$ and that $\frac{1}{2}mv_\perp{}^2 = L^2/2mr^2$.)

P11.11 (1) (Note that B is the "binding energy" of the rocket near the earth and that E + B is the initial kinetic energy of the rocket.)
(2) 1. $\theta = 0$: The path is a straight radial line ($b = 0$) for all E. 2. $\theta \neq 0$: As $E \to 0$, the path approaches a parabola and $b \to \infty$ (the speed at great distance approaches zero). As $E \to \infty$, the path approaches a straight line and $b \to R \sin\theta$.

P11.12 (2) $U_{eff} = \dfrac{L^2}{2mr^2} - \dfrac{GmM_E}{r}$.

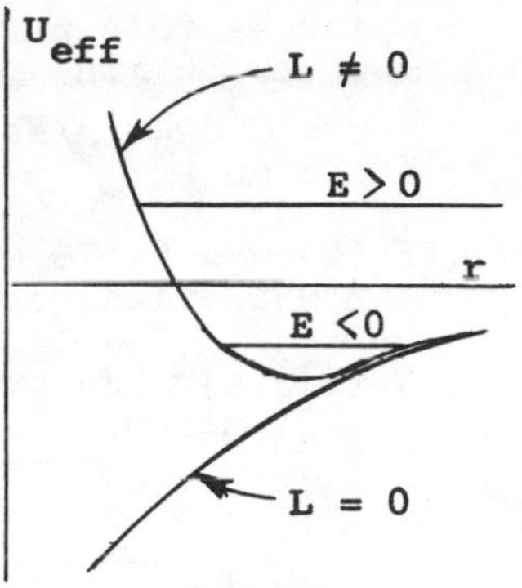

(3) Define $a = GmM_E/2|E|$, $b = L/\sqrt{2m|E|}$, $c = \sqrt{a^2 - b^2}$. For $E < 0$, $r_{min} = a - \sqrt{a^2 - b^2} = a - c$, $r_{max} = a + \sqrt{a^2 - b^2} = a + c$ (a and b are the semimajor and semiminor axes of the elliptical orbit). For $E > 0$, $r_{min} = -a + \sqrt{a^2 + b^2}$ (a and b are the parameters of the hyperbolic orbit as defined in Exercise 11.35).

(4) $E = -m(GmM_E)^2/2L^2$.

P11.13 (1) $U = -\dfrac{GmM_E}{r} - \dfrac{GmM_M}{r_m - r}$. (3) U is maximum at $r_o = r_m/(1 + \sqrt{\gamma})$, where $\gamma = M_M/M_E = 0.01229$. (This can also be written $r_o = r_m[\xi - \sqrt{\xi^2 - \xi}]$, where $\xi = M_E/(M_E - M_M) = 1/(1 - \gamma) = 1.0124$.)

The numerical value is $r_o = 0.900 r_m = 3.46 \times 10^8$ m. The distance of this point from the center of the moon is $r_m - r_o = r_m\sqrt{\gamma}/(1 + \sqrt{\gamma}) = 0.100 r_m = 3.84 \times 10^7$ m. $U_{max} = -\dfrac{GmM_E}{r_m}(1 + \sqrt{\gamma})^2 = -\dfrac{GmM_E}{r_o}(1 + \sqrt{\gamma})$. In terms of potential energy at the earth's surface, it is $U_{max} = -\dfrac{GmM_E}{R}\left[\dfrac{R}{r_m}(1 + \sqrt{\gamma})^2\right] = 0.0204U(R) = U(R)/49$.

(4) $v_{esc} - v'_{esc} = \sqrt{\dfrac{2GM_E}{R}}\left[1 - \sqrt{1 - \dfrac{R}{r_m}(1 + \sqrt{\gamma})^2}\right]$

$= 0.0103 v_{esc} = 115$ m/sec.

P11.15 (1) $a = 0.0238$ m/sec^2 $= 0.00243g = g/411$. For most purposes, this acceleration can be ignored.
(2) 0.098 deg, or 0.00171 radian. [These numbers are calculated using 24 hr as an approximation for

the earth's period. The correct sidereal period, 23 hr 56 min, yields slightly different answers: $a = 0.0240$ m/sec^2 and $\theta = 0.099$ deg $= 0.00173$ radian.]

P11.16 (a) $a = 6{,}378$ km $= 3{,}963$ miles; $b = 6{,}357$ km $= 3{,}950$ miles.

P11.17 (2) $|z| \ll 2a$ or $|z| \ll (a/b)|x|$. (4) 8.55 km, or 5.31 miles.

P11.18 ($\ell_1' = \sqrt{\ell_1^2 + s^2 + 2\ell_1 s \cos\theta_1}$,

$\ell_2' = \sqrt{\ell_2^2 + s^2 - 2\ell_2 s \cos\theta_2}$.

$d(\ell_1' + \ell_2')/ds \rightarrow \cos\theta_1 - \cos\theta_2$ as $s \rightarrow 0$.)

P11.19 $y = 2\ell - x$ (a straight line).

P11.21 (2) $v_b/v_a = 2$, $v_p/v_a = 4$. (3) The gain of speed is greater in going from B to P.

P11.22 (2)

Point	Ratio K/U
A	$-\frac{1}{2}(1 - e)$
B	$-\frac{1}{2}$
P	$-\frac{1}{2}(1 + e)$

P11.23 $n > 2$: The axis rotates in the same direction as the rotation of the planet in its orbit.
$n < 2$: The axis rotates opposite to the direction of rotation of the planet in its orbit. [For $n > 2$, the force varies more rapidly with radius than an inverse-square force. Relative to the inverse-square force, this force can be considered to be stronger at perigee and weaker at apogee. For $n < 2$, the force, relative to an inverse-square force, may be considered to be weaker at perigee and stronger at apogee because it varies less rapidly with radius.]

P11.24 (1) $F \sim 1/r^5$. (2) Yes. $F \sim r$, or $F_r \sim -r$ (a two-dimensional harmonic oscillator).

P11.25 (1) Number 5 missing. Should be at about 2.7 to 2.8 A.U. (2) $B = 0.074$ A.U. (reasonable range 0.072 to 0.076). (3) Yes.

P11.26 (1)(a) $U_{\parallel} = -\frac{GmM_E}{r_0}\left[\frac{1}{1-\varepsilon} + \frac{1}{1+\varepsilon}\right] \cong$

$-\frac{2GmM_E}{r_o}(1+\varepsilon^2)$. (b) $U_\perp = -\frac{2GmM_E}{r_o}\frac{1}{\sqrt{1+\varepsilon^2}} \cong -\frac{2GmM_E}{r_o}(1-\frac{1}{2}\varepsilon^2)$. (2) The orientation parallel to a radial line has lower potential energy (more negative). (3) $\overline{T} = \frac{6}{\pi}\frac{GmM_E}{r_o}\varepsilon^2 = \frac{6}{\pi}\frac{GmM_E a^2}{r_o^3}$.

(4) The moon must have a nonuniform mass distribution analogous to that of the satellite. Over eons, tidal effects have damped out the oscillation that would normally occur about the angle of least potential energy. <u>Optional</u>:

$$U = -\frac{GmM_E}{r_o}\left(\frac{1}{\sqrt{1-2\varepsilon\cos\theta+\varepsilon^2}} + \frac{1}{\sqrt{1+2\varepsilon\cos\theta+\varepsilon^2}}\right),$$

$U \cong -(2GmM_E/r_o)\left[1+\frac{1}{2}\varepsilon^2(3\cos^2\theta-1)\right]$, where θ is the angle between the satellite axis and the radial line. The magnitude of the torque is $T = |dU/d\theta| = (6GmM_E/r_o)\varepsilon^2\cos\theta\sin\theta$.

P11.27 (2) S_2 lags by $3\pi\Delta r$ along its orbit, so that in one revolution, the distance between S_1 and S_2 grows from Δr to $\sqrt{9\pi^2+1}\,\Delta r$, or $9.48\Delta r$. The result is independent of r_1 (but assumes $\Delta r \ll r_1$).

(2) S_2 lags by 37.7 m along its orbit; its distance from S_1 grows from 4 m to 37.9 m.

(3) No. (The initial acceleration of each satellite toward the other is 4.17×10^{-9} m/sec^2. If their relative velocity were zero initially and they were not influenced by the earth, this acceleration would decrease their separation by 0.12 m in 90 min. But because their orbits cause them to move apart, the force between them diminishes and the net effect of their attraction will amount to no more than about 0.01 m in one revolution.)

P11.28 (2) The apogee of S_2's orbit is at $r_1 + 3\Delta r$. When S_2 is at apogee, S_1 has moved through half a circle plus an extra distance $3\pi\Delta r$: S_2 is then $3\Delta r$ <u>below</u> S_1 and $3\pi\Delta r$ <u>ahead</u> of S_1. Their total separation is $3\Delta r\sqrt{1+\pi^2}$, or $9.89\Delta r$. (3) S_1 is 12 m below S_2 and

37.7 m ahead of S_2. Their total separation is 39.6 m. [Note: The formula given in Problem 10.21 is useful here.]

P11.29 [Optional part: Along a line from the center to point 1, the contact force needed to support the particle is $F_1' = (mgr/R)[1 - (3R\omega^2)/g]$, where r is the distance from the center (note that the fractional correction to mgr/R is independent of r). Along a line from the center to point 3, the required contact force is $F_3' = mgr/R$. The difference in work is $W_3 - W_1 = (3/2)mR^2\omega^2$. Unusually able students may wish to verify that this difference in potential energy between points 1 and 3 can also be obtained by considering the work required to move a particle along the surface of the spherical earth from point 1 to point 3. Problem: At an arbitrary point 4 located on the surface between points 1 and 3, show that the horizontal component of the contact force is $F_{4x} = -mg\cos\theta\,[1 - (3R\omega^2/g)]$, the vertical component of the contact force is $F_{4y} = mg\sin\theta$, and the component parallel to the surface is $F_{\parallel} = 3mR\omega^2\sin\theta\cos\theta$ (θ is the angular separation of points 4 and 1). The work required to move the particle from point 1 to point 3 is then $W = R\int_0^{\pi/2} F_{\parallel}\,d\theta = (3/2)mR^2\omega^2$. This method shows more clearly that a tidal force acts to move the oceans parallel to the earth's surface. The method can be generalized to a nonspherical rotating earth.]

CHAPTER 12

Q12.1 (1) The coefficient of friction between the tires and the surface sets the limit (e.g., for $\mu_s = 1$, $a_{max} = g$). (2) A vehicle driven by an airplane engine and propeller or by a jet engine.

Q12.2 For $\tan\theta < \mu_s$, the block is motionless. For $\mu_s < \tan\theta < \mu_k$, the block might execute stop-and-start motion down the plank with low average speed and zero average acceleration. For $\tan\theta > \mu_k$, the block accelerates down the plank with $a = g\sin\theta - \mu_k g\cos\theta = g\cos\theta\,(\tan\theta - \mu_k)$.

Q12.3 (1) B is most likely loose material. C is most likely hard material. (2) For part B, $\mu_s = 1$.

Q12.4 It does not prove Equation 12.4. (Characteristic angles of repose would result from almost any law of friction.)

Q12.5 Disturbing vibrations, for example, or feeding the pile at points other than its apex.

Q12.6 The coefficient of static friction. To good approximation, there is no relative motion of tire and road.

Q12.7 Definition: the force needed to keep a vehicle rolling at constant speed on a horizontal surface (after correction for air resistance, if any) divided by the vehicle's weight.

Q12.10 In a uniform gravitational field, the force and torque produced by gravity can be duplicated by a single force acting at the center of mass of the system (the theorem stated on page 492 of the text).

Q12.11 (1) (Apply the theorem stated on page 492 of the text; put the origin at the center of mass.) (2) Gravity does not alter the spin angular momentum of a falling body or projectile.

Q12.13 [Ingenious students can probably think of a variety of methods. One simple method is to use the envelope itself as a lever: Let a ruler or the edge of a book act as a fulcrum supporting the envelope along a line that does not pass through the center of the envelope, and use the spring balance to hold up the heavier end. Note that any method that brings another lever into play must take account of the weight of the lever.]

Q12.15 (1) (The answer should call attention to the fact that in liquids molecules are "closely packed"—molecular diameter and mean distance between molecular centers being comparable.)

Q12.16 Viscosity (a measure of the ability of the liquid to sustain shear forces).

Q12.17 An element of fluid is <u>pulling</u> rather than <u>pushing</u> on its surroundings.

Q17.18 It minimizes its potential energy by minimizing its surface area (a surface tension effect).

Q12.19 Two advantages of mercury: a low vapor pressure (the region above the column of liquid remains at very low pressure) and a high density (the column is not excessively long). Water is much less satisfactory on both counts.

Q12.20 It is harder to suck through a longer straw and harder to suck a denser liquid (see the second term on the right side of Equation 12.30).

Q12.21 (1) Yes—at least to good approximation. (2) No.

Q12.22 (Archimedes' principle is applied. The ship's horizontal cross-sectional area must be known as a function of distance from the keel.)

Q12.23 (1) Slightly lower average density.
(2) Salt water is denser than fresh water.
(3) Air in the lungs lowers the average density.
(4) No.

Q12.24 $v \sim 1/d^2$.

Q12.25 Yes, in principle, if the density varies in inverse proportion to the cross-sectional area ($\rho \sim 1/A$).

Q12.26 (1) Yes, if steady flow is defined as flow in which conditions at each point are independent of time. (2) Yes. (3) No.

Q12.27 Its speed increases, so its cross-sectional area decreases (Av = constant). [See also Problems 12.18 and 12.19.]

Q12.28 If it has broken into a myriad of droplets or if it is at terminal speed. For the first possibility, it is compressible; for the second possibility, it could be incompressible. For both possibilities, the equation of continuity is valid. [See also Problem 12.19.]

Q12.29 (1) The speed is greatest where the streamlines are closest together: above the leading edge of the airfoil (its left edge) and below its trailing edge. The speed is least where the streamlines are most widely separated: above and behind the trailing edge. (2) The pressure is greatest where the speed is least; the pressure is least where the speed is greatest.

Q12.30 Air density would be needed. It could be obtained from air pressure and temperature (so additional input from a barometer and a thermometer would be needed).

Q12.31 Cavitation is the formation of gas-filled or vapor-filled cavities in a flowing liquid. It would normally invalidate both equations because the flow would not be steady. Under special conditions, flow with cavitation can be approximated as steady flow. The equations could then be used with <u>average</u> values of compressibility and density for the liquid-vapor mixture.

Q12.32 No. It would fall with constant acceleration. Its rate of dissipation of heat energy would grow without limit.

Q12.33 No. It is not path-independent. (Note in particular that the net work done by this force is not zero around a closed path.)

Q12.34 Both vary approximately in proportion to v^2. [See also Problem 12.20.]

Q12.35 (a) The sphere of smaller radius.
(b) The sphere of greater mass.
(c) The sphere of greater mass and radius.

Q12.36 Paraffin contains hydrogen. Neutrons readily transfer energy to protons in hydrogen. Neutrons lose very little energy in elastic collisions with lead nuclei. [See also Problems 12.28 and 12.31.]

Q12.37 The minimum relative speed is zero. The maximum relative speed is $2\sqrt{2K_1/m}$ (twice the speed of the particle in either frame).

Q12.38 The density of particles in a beam is much less than in a solid target. Interaction events per unit volume per unit time are less in colliding beams.

. . . .

E12.1 (1) 38.7 deg, or 0.675 radian (arc tan 0.8).
(2) 0.156g, or 1.53 m/sec^2. (3) 1.75 m/sec.

E12.2 $0.3 < \mu_s$ (child) < 0.4, μ_s(man) > 0.4.

E12.4 (1) Initially, $a > \mu_s g$. Continuing, $a > \mu_k g$.
(2) None, except insofar as it influences the entertainer's ability to pull with sufficient force.
(3) He or she is likely to allow the acceleration to decrease below the critical value $\mu_k g$ after a certain speed is attained.

E12.10 (1) $F_f = mg(s/L)\text{ctn}\,\theta$ (or $mg(s/y)\cos\theta$).
(2) 1.819 m.

E12.11 $(\mu_s)_{min} = 0.328$ ($= 0.9\ \text{ctn}\,\theta$).

E12.12 (1) 9.8 N. (2) 9.8 N m relative to one end of the pole (9.31 N m relative to the midpoint of his grasp). (3) A force of 88.2 N acting downward at the end of the pole and a force of 98 N acting upward 0.1 m from the end of the pole.

E12.13 F_1 = 1,537 N. F_2 = 1,250 N.

E12.14 F_3 = 1,700 N. F_4 = 1,300 N.

E12.15 1.262.

E12.16 $F_A = F_C$ = 1,414 N, F_B = 672 N.

E12.17 (1) $F_{gx} = 0$, F_{gy} = - 196 N; F_{1x} = - 130.7 N, F_{1y} = 98 N; F_{2x} = 130.7 N, F_{2y} = 98 N.
(2) 0.75.

E12.18 4.36×10^5 N/m^2, or 4.31 atm.

E12.19 (1) It increases gradually from 1.097 atm to 10.097 atm (1.111×10^5 N/m^2 to 1.023×10^6 N/m^2).
(2) The same as part 1.

E12.20 (a) 10.34 m. (b) 8.55 m (based on p = 0.827 atm; the assumed scale height is 8 km).

E12.21 (1) 2.478×10^4 N. (2) 2.431×10^4 N.
(3) 470 N, directed outward. (This force is $\frac{1}{2}\rho g h^2 \ell$, where $\rho = 10^3$ kg/m^3, h = 0.4 m, and ℓ = 0.6 m.)

E12.22 (1) 0.683 (i.e. to 68.3 percent of the sea-level value, or less by a factor of 1.46).
(2) 0.264 (26.4 percent of the sea-level value, or less by a factor of 3.79). [The calculations use an assumed scale height of 8 km.]

E12.23 (1) $\alpha = p_0/b$. (2) 3.8 percent (for b = 8 km).

E12.24 Absolute: within 77 N/m^2 at sea level, decreasing to 64 N/m^2 at 5,000 ft. Relative: 0.076 percent (1 part in 1,310) at sea level, decreasing to 0.063 percent (1 part in 1,590) at 5,000 ft. Rough average values: 70 N/m^2 absolute and 0.07 percent relative.

E12.25 (1) 600 kg/m^3 (0.6 gm/cm^3). (2) Yes. About 14 percent (for ρ(gasoline) = 700 kg/m^3).

E12.26 75 percent.

E12.27 (1) 6,000 kg/m^3 (6 gm/cm^3). (2) 2.7 N.

E12.28 (1) 4.9882 N. (2) 5.0118 N. (3) 5.000 N.
[Note: These answers assume $\rho(\text{air}) = 1.20\ kg/m^3$. For air at standard conditions with $\rho = 1.293\ kg/m^3$, the answers to parts 1 and 2 would be 4.9873 N and 5.0127 N.

E12.29 F = 490 N, directed downward. $a = 0.248\ m/sec^2$ = 0.0253g.

E12.30 (1) 2.25. (2) 1 (no change).

E12.31 3.33. Does not require constant temperature.

E12.33 (1) $1.013 \times 10^5\ J/m^3$. (2) 101.3 J/kg.

E12.34 (1) 3.675 m/sec. (2) 2.040 atm, or $2.067 \times 10^5\ N/m^2$.

E12.35 $1.018 \times 10^5\ N/m^2$, or 1.0053 atm (for $\rho(\text{air}) = 1.2\ kg/m^3$).

E12.36 v = 396 m/sec = Mach 1.2.

E12.37 (1) $3.95 \times 10^5\ N/m^2$, or 3.90 atm.
(2) $5.0 \times 10^4\ N/m^2$, or 0.494 atm.
(3) 13.5 m/sec. (4) 0.307 m.

E12.38 (1) 20.1 m/sec. (2) 0.1027 kg. (F = 1.006 N.)

E12.39 (2) $C = (dm/dt)^2/2\rho$. (3) (The maximum pressure p_1 is approached as $A \to \infty$ (and $v \to 0$). The minimum pressure p = 0 is reached at a critical area $A_c = \sqrt{C/p_1}$. For $A < A_c$, steady flow cannot persist.)

E12.40 The speed does not change.

E12.41 (1) $R = 2\sqrt{y(h - y)}$. It is the same on the moon.

E12.42 (1) 2,160 N/m^2, or 0.0213 atm, for $\rho(\text{air}) = 1.20\ kg/m^3$ (2,327 N/m^2, or 0.0230 atm, for $\rho(\text{air}) = 1.293\ kg/m^3$). (2) 72.6 m/sec (for $\rho/\rho_0 = 0.683$, based on a scale height of 8 km).

E12.44 (1) 1.83. (2) 2.98.

E12.45 (1) $P \sim v^3$. (2) (P is more nearly proportional to v^2 than to v^3. The drag coefficient of the airplanes must decrease as their power and speed increase.)

(3) In the order listed, 1.00/0.889/0.711/0.505, or 1.98/1.76/1.41/1.00.

E12.47 (1) Reasonable range about 50 to 75 m/sec, or 110 to 170 mile/hr. (2) About 125 to 290 m.

E12.49 The smaller sphere has twice the density of the larger sphere.

E12.50 (1) $v_T = mg/6\pi\mu r$.

E12.51 Dimensionless.

E12.52 (1) 0 to 0.0075 m/sec for $\rho(\text{air}) = 1.2\ \text{kg/m}^3$ (to 0.0070 m/sec for $\rho(\text{air}) = 1.293\ \text{kg/m}^3$).
(2) 0.225 to 225 m/sec for $\rho(\text{air}) = 1.2\ \text{kg/m}^3$ (0.208 to 208 m/sec for $\rho(\text{air}) = 1.293\ \text{kg/m}^3$).

E12.53 (1) $v_T = 0.052$ m/sec; $R = 10$. (2) Of order 10^{-2} sec. (The characteristic time is $t_0 = v_T/g = 0.0053$ sec. Reasonable range of estimates: $2t_0$ to $10t_0$.) [Exact solution: $t = -t_0 \ln[1 - (v/v_T)]$. The time to reach $0.9v_T$ is $2.30t_0$, or 0.012 sec. The time to reach $0.99v_T$ is $4.61t_0$, or 0.024 sec.]

E12.54 (1)(a) 0.75 MeV. (b) 0.50 MeV. (c) 0.25 MeV. (2) 10.

E12.55 Angle of proton track, 56.8 deg (arc sin $\sqrt{0.7}$). Deflection angle of neutron, 33.2 deg (arc cos $\sqrt{0.7}$). (These angles in radians are 0.991 and 0.580.)

E12.57 (1) 9.23 MeV. (2) 0.77 MeV. (3) 5 MeV. (4) 20 MeV.

. . . .

P12.1 (3) $F_{min} = 4\mu mg$. $F_{max} = 8\mu mg$.

P12.4 (1) ($\mathbf{F} \perp d\mathbf{s}$. $W = 0$.) (2) A vertical force can lift the block free of the plank so that work need be done only against gravity, not against friction.

P12.5 124 m. ($s = (\mu^{-1} \sin\theta - \cos\theta)\ell$, where $\ell = 50$ m.)

P12.6 9.43×10^{-4}. ($\mu = \tan\theta \dfrac{0.95s_1 - s_2}{0.95s_1 + s_2}$; with $s_1 = 2$ m and $s_2 = 1.8$ m, this becomes $\mu = \tan\theta/37 \cong \sin\theta/37 \cong \theta/37$.)

P12.7 (1) $v_{min} = \sqrt{rg/\mu}$. (2) 18.1 mile/hr. (3) arc tan (gr/v^2). (4) Downward, or to the motorcyclist's left in the diagram. (Consider a plane defined by the motorcycle's wheels if the front wheel is <u>not</u> turned. Just ahead of the motorcycle, the intersection of this plane with the cylinder is a rising curve. The cyclist would move up this rising curve if he did not turn his wheel.)

P12.8 He should ride on the beam 3.5 m from its left end (1.5 m from its right end). (Then F_1 = 1,537 N, F_2 = 1,250 N, and $F_3 = F_4$ = 2,000 N. If he rode on the load, both F_1 and F_3 would exceed 2,000 N. If he rode at any other point on the beam, either F_3 or F_4 would exceed 2,000 N.)

P12.9 $F_c = F_t = mg/\sqrt{3} = 0.577mg$. [It is convenient to consider the equilibrium of one sloping beam and to choose an origin at either end of this beam. The vertical forces that act on a sloping beam are (a) 1.5mg, upward at its lower end; (b) 1.0mg, downward at its center; and (c) 0.5mg, downward at its upper end. The horizontal forces that act on this beam are the oppositely directed forces F_c and F_t.]

P12.10 (2) Sample values of F/N for no slipping:

θ (deg)	F/N
30	0.3464
40	0.5082
50	0.5519
60	0.4786

[For $\mu_s = 0.5$, slipping occurs for 39.3 deg $\lesssim \theta \lesssim$ 58.0 deg.]

P12.12 (2) (For $y \ll R$, the approximation of Equation 12.30 is valid—a linear dependence of p on y. For $y \gg R$, the pressure approaches a constant, $p \cong p_0 - \rho g_0 R$.) (3) On earth the fractional error is 4.71×10^{-6} (1 part in 212,000). On the small planet, the approximately calculated pressure difference is larger than the true pressure difference by 30 percent. (p(approx)/p(actual) = 1.30, p(actual)/p(approx) = 0.769.)

P12.13 (1) $p = p_0 - \rho g_0 y[1 - (y/R)]$.

P12.14 (2) Equation 12.30 with $g = g_0$ slightly <u>overestimates</u> the pressure. [Equation 12.30 with $g = g_0(R - d)/R$ slightly <u>underestimates</u> the pressure. In early printings of the text, the wording of the problem is ambiguous and permits either answer.] (3) 7.84×10^7 N/m^2, or 773 atm. The correction factor $1 - (d/2R)$ differs from 1 by 0.06 percent, which is insignificant for most purposes.

P12.15 $\rho = \dfrac{\rho_0}{[1 + (y/b)]^2}$, $p = \dfrac{p_0}{1 + (y/b)}$,

where $b = p_0/\rho_0 g$. [Note that the characteristic length b has the same form as in a "Boyle's law" exponential atmosphere: see Equation 12.40.]

P12.17 (1) [Note that the answer requires a cylindrical <u>shape</u> (constant cross-sectional area) but does <u>not</u> require a uniform density of the rod.]
(2) ω depends only indirectly on the density of the liquid. As the density of the liquid increases, s_0 decreases and ω increases. (If the rod is of uniform density, $s_0 \sim 1/\rho(\text{liquid})$ and $\omega \sim \sqrt{\rho(\text{liquid})}$.)

P12.18 $d = \dfrac{D}{[1 + (2gs/v_0^2)]^{\frac{1}{4}}}$; d is the diameter of the stream, s is the distance below the faucet.

P12.19 (1) [Note: Only a qualitative answer is called for.] (2) (The "density" of the water—actually of the air-water mixture—is given by $\rho = \rho_0 v_0/v$. It approaches $\rho_T = \rho_0 v_0/v_T$, where v_T is the terminal speed of the droplets. (The area of the stream is assumed constant.) When terminal speed is reached, v_0/v_T is the fraction of the volume of the stream occupied by water; $1 - (v_0/v_T)$ is the fraction occupied by air.) (3) The speed rises from v_0 and approaches a constant v_T. The density of a droplet remains constant (ρ_0). The average density of many droplets decreases from ρ_0 and approaches a constant $\rho_T = \rho_0 v_0/v_T$. The average spacing between droplets rises from zero and approaches a constant value.

P12.20 (1) Net pressure $p_2 - p_1 = \frac{1}{2}\rho v_0^2[(A_0/A_1)^2 - (A_0/A_2)^2]$. (2) 703 N/m^2. (On a wing area of 15 m^2, this net pressure produces a lift force of about 10,000 N, sufficient to lift about 1,000 kg, or 2,200 lb. These figures are the right order of magnitude for light planes.) (3) A requirement of Newton's second and third laws. The wing must push downward on the air and give it a downward component of momentum.

P12.21 (1) Excess pressure $\cong \rho \ell v/\Delta t$. (2) 2.5 atm. [Note: This simple treatment overestimates the excess pressure because it ignores friction in the pipe and assumes that all the force exerted by the decelerating water is exerted at the faucet valve.]

P12.22 (1) Input power: $P_1 = F_1 v_1 = p_1 A_1 v_1$. Output power: $P_2 = F_2 v_2 = p_2 A_2 v_2$. Net rate of change of kinetic energy of fluid: $dK/dt = \frac{1}{2}(dm/dt)(v_2{}^2 - v_1{}^2)$, where $dm/dt = \rho A_1 v_1 = \rho A_2 v_2$. The equation $P_1 = P_2 + dK/dt$ reduces to Bernoulli's equation (Equation 12.60) because of the equality $A_1 v_1 = A_2 v_2$ (Equation 12.49).

P12.23 (1) $n \cong 3$. ($n = \ln(3/2)/\ln(32/28) = 3.04$.) (2) 4.85 m, or 15.9 ft.

P12.24 Equivalent ways to express the work:

$$W = \tfrac{1}{2}C_D A \rho v_T{}^2[\ell - x_c(1 - e^{-\ell/x_c})]$$

$$= \tfrac{1}{2}(mv_T{}^2/x_c)[\ell - x_c(1 - e^{-\ell/x_c})]$$

$$= mg[\ell - x_c(1 - e^{-\ell/x_c})]$$

$$= mg\ell - \tfrac{1}{2}mv_T{}^2(1 - e^{-\ell/x_c}).$$

(See Equations 12.69 and 12.76 for definitions of v_T and x_c.)

P12.25 $F_D = \frac{1}{2}A\rho v_0{}^2$. $C_D = 1$. [The A. I. P. Handbook, first edition (New York: McGraw-Hill Book Co., Inc., 1957), page 2-188, gives $C_D = 0.8$ for a disk without cavitation and $C_D > 0.8$ for a disk with cavitation.]

P12.26 $F_D = \frac{1}{2}A\rho v^2$. $C_D = 1$. <u>Optional</u>: The method is equivalent to the method in Problem 12.25.

P12.28 (1) Most probable angle, 45 deg ($\pi/4$). Least probable angles, 0 and 90 deg ($\pi/2$). (Deflection angles greater than 90 deg do not occur.) (2) $\Delta K = \frac{1}{2}K_0$. (3) $dN/d\psi \sim \sin\psi$ ($0 \leq \psi \leq \pi$).

P12.29 (a) $\underset{\sim}{p}_1 = \underset{\sim}{p}_0 - mV\underset{\sim}{i}$, $K_1 = K_0 + \frac{1}{2}mV^2 - Vp_{0x}$.

(b) $\underset{\sim}{p}_1 = (p_0 - mV)\underset{\sim}{i}$, $K_1 = K_0 + \frac{1}{2}mV^2 - Vp_0 = (p_0 - mV)^2/2m$. (This can also be written $K_1 = (\sqrt{K_0} - \sqrt{\widetilde{K}})^2$, where $\widetilde{K} = \frac{1}{2}mV^2$.)

P12.30 (2) It is more likely to escape. The speed $2v_M$ exceeds the escape speed from the earth for a body starting at the distance of the moon (this escape speed is $\sqrt{2}\,v_M$). (3) (To gain much speed, the spacecraft must be deflected through a large angle. If its initial speed v_1 is too great, it cannot experience a large-angle deflection because of the finite radius of the moon or planet. So the faster it is moving initially, the less speed it can gain in a single pass. Also, the faster it is moving initially, the more difficult it would be to produce a change of direction at one moon or planet that would carry the craft to another moon or planet.)

P12.31 (1) $mv_0 = mv_1 \cos\theta + Mv_2 \cos\varphi$,

$$0 = mv_1 \sin\theta - Mv_2 \sin\varphi,$$

$$\tfrac{1}{2}mv_0{}^2 = \tfrac{1}{2}mv_1{}^2 + \tfrac{1}{2}Mv_2{}^2.$$

(3) The + sign is required to make $v_1 > 0$. The maximum deflection angle is 180 deg (π). The maximum fractional loss of energy is 8/9. For $\theta = 45$ deg, the fractional loss of energy is $(5 - \sqrt{17})/9$, or 0.262.

A B C D E F G 7 6 5 4 3 2